Unlocking the skills that will define success in an evolving world

CHARLIE BOYLE

The Future is Human

ISBN 978-1-915483-74-4

eISBN 978-1-915483-75-1

Published in 2025 by Right Book Press

Printed in the UK in May 2025

Manufactured by
Sue Richardson Associates Ltd.
Studio 6,
9, Marsh Street
Bristol
BS1 4AA

info@therightbookcompany.com

EU Safety Representative
eucomply OÜ
Parnu mnt 139b-14
11317 Tallinn
Estonia

hello@eucompliancepartner.com
+33 756 90241

© Charlie Boyle

The right of Charlie Boyle to be identified as the author of this work has been asserted in accordance with the Copyright, Designs and Patents Act 1988.

A CIP record of this book is available from the British Library.

All rights reserved. No part of this book may be reproduced, stored in a retrieval system, or transmitted in any form or by any means, electronic, mechanical, photocopying, recording or otherwise, without the prior written permission of the copyright holder.

While technology advances at breakneck speed, this book convincingly argues that our human qualities become more essential, not less. Charlie Boyle weaves place, people and purpose into compelling narratives and emerges as one of our era's most gifted voices, offering vignettes that illuminate core human capabilities. For anyone navigating our increasingly automated future, this thought leader provides a practical roadmap for thriving by mastering the most powerful technology of all – our humanity.
– **Katie McMahon**, tech executive and AI product pioneer, formerly VP at Shazam, SoundHound AI

Charlie Boyle has tapped into two important insights in this wonderful book. The first is that your people really are your most valuable resource, and that investment in human skills will have the single biggest impact on business success. The second is that the timeless art of storytelling is a wonderful educational tool that helps us understand, engage with and remember the key learnings.
– **Dr Deirdre Curran**, lecturer, researcher and vice dean of Equality, Diversity & Inclusion at the University of Galway

One of the major unintended consequences from increasing digitalisation has been the atrophy of human skills. This must-read book masterfully illustrates how to reaffirm these 'lost' skills and keep pace with technological changes.
– **Dr Mark J. McGinley**, author of *Critical Relief: A CEO's Guide to Transforming Hospital Culture*

This book explores how our interactions with people throughout our lives influence our leadership style and values, and how we can best connect these human skills to the world of business. A warm, honest and sincerely thought-provoking read.
– **Lisa Fallon**, FIFA Global Football Development Division

Charlie Boyle is a master storyteller who captures the beauty of the smallest detail, the warmth of community and the value of resilience. Reading this book will benefit everyone: people who want to pursue excellence in business and leadership, employers who want to gain a deeper insight into customer intention or just the curious reader.
– **Joe McHugh TD**, former Irish Minister for Education

Contents

Introduction	1
1. Connecting through storytelling	9
2. Community building and social impact	17
3. Psychological safety	27
4. Leadership	35
5. Accountability	47
6. Diversity	57
7. Emotional intelligence	65
8. Dealing with ambiguity	73
9. Conflict management	85
10. Teamwork	93
11. Growth mindset	105
12. Effective communication	113
13. Vision and values	123
14. Stress management	133
15. Empathy	139
16. Compassion	147
17. Creativity and design thinking	157
18. Cross-cultural understanding	167
19. Resilience	173
20. Collaboration	183
Summary: The Irish wake, the greatest show on Earth	193
Acknowledgements	199
Bibliography	205

Introduction

I've always been fascinated by people. In my childhood and youth, I could seldom articulate why, but came to understand it more during my working life. I have a hunger to explore why people behave in the ways they do, and how even those of opposite personalities can complement each other when they use different skills. I would later study human skills academically yet always be drawn back to examples much closer to home. This curiosity would much later involve a working trip to the renowned Massachusetts Institute of Technology (MIT) and even more intrigue and questions about the importance of human skills – essentially, human abilities and traits that are difficult to replicate with technology – in the modern world of digitally driven business.

The origin of this book and the inspiration to study human skills and their impact on customer experience are rooted in my home region of West Donegal and have grown through the twists and turns my life has taken since I moved to the area with my parents as a young boy. I've had the privilege of encountering characters and players of all kinds – shopkeepers, community leaders, teachers, football managers and business managers. Many were people of the highest integrity and had all the traits of compassionate leaders. They have inspired me in some way throughout my life.

While I was involved in pub management during a 13-year period in London from 1997 to 2010, the structure and strategies I used during this time proved to be successful and led to sales growth as well as national and international sales awards. It was always a team effort but the system I followed worked in the pub industry. I often wanted to look back at the successes of that period and examine the practices that worked well. Years later, I had that chance while doing a master's in leadership and innovation. This helped me to understand that business is ultimately about people and those who succeed have a high level of human skills, which can be gifted from birth but also developed through learning.

I founded Customer Service Excellence Ireland (CSEI) in 2014. It has been an interesting business that, like all businesses, has had its challenges. However, in recent years, the company has enjoyed many achievements and employed three full-time and three part-time staff, with the team carrying out work in several sectors to improve customer experience. We have delivered programmes at Tesco Ireland, Applegreen, Brown Thomas, Lidl, Circle K, Aramark, Boots and McDonalds, as well as a five-year programme with Fáilte Ireland (Irish Tourist Board). CSEI has also carried out contracts with civil engineering businesses in the UK, shopping centres, Dubai Islamic Bank and Ireland's Department of Justice. CSEI continues to attract requests and tenders on interesting projects that are a joy to be involved in.

In 2018, I was appointed by Ireland's Educational

Training Board to help create a national professional sales apprenticeship. A big part of my role and responsibility was to ask Irish employers what type of people they needed in their sales teams. A trend quickly emerged. Businesses felt that the sales and marketing graduates coming to them after four years of studying for a degree were well educated in theory and academic work, but lacked the social or human skills required for the workplace. Google, Microsoft and other leading tech companies with a European base in Dublin told me they were suspending the requirement of a degree and replacing it with direct recruitment from secondary school to allow for a more practical and pragmatic education pathway of work-based learning.

By this time, I was combining raw observations of the personalities who shaped my local community in West Donegal with the academic study in which I was engrossed. I was most fascinated by the fact that, even without qualifications or the credibility of accredited courses, there was an abundance of talent – people who naturally exhibited high levels of leadership, empathy, compassion, collaboration and other key human skills and traits, with innovation and often failure included as vital ingredients of their success.

A 2020 report from Skillnet Ireland (which was driven by two good people, Dr Oran Doherty and Roisin Woods) highlighted the rising need for human skills in retail, Ireland's largest sectoral employer. I was asked to contribute to this report and again, I came across a strong requirement from employers to highlight the gap in human skills that was now emerging as a regular topic.

Research carried out in the US at MIT over the past

six years suggests that at least 50 per cent of the essential workplace skills of the future will be human skills. The contradiction or problem (which is also the opportunity) is that human skills are not being included in learning, skills and development programmes proportionate to the need for them.

In 2022, Dr Doherty and I were invited to join MIT's research project. With the open invitation of a trip to Boston and strong encouragement from the recognised thought leader, George Westerman, who is based there, I was asked to chair a global opportunity initiative on human skills. This was an unexpected honour and one that I was thoroughly excited about. It presented me with a chance to be part of something I believe in, to learn from others and create change. I felt as if I was being given the opportunity to further democratise education.

Education must disrupt itself or be disrupted. It has been far too slow to innovate. Universities and third-level institutions do an enormous amount of good and will continue to do so. I've availed myself of their excellence, as have my family and friends. However, the system has, in many ways, fallen behind the fast-changing needs of our world. Many current degrees of three to four years' duration will be replaced by micro-credentials. Lifelong learning will replace the current norm of a one-off education during the late teens and early twenties. Apprenticeships will become more common and will expand into new areas.

I want to be involved in a movement that puts human skills at its foundation in terms of who we are and what we do as educators, business innovators and people.

Introduction

The twists and turns of my life have transformed me from being a person with negative thought patterns into someone who values compassion, accountability and cross-cultural understanding. By practising these skills, among others, I'm the benefactor of improved relationships in the workplace and outside of it. I care deeply about persuading organisations to go deeper and to treat people better. I want to help change the internal culture of organisations so that employees feel valued as people and collaboration between and within businesses is used to improve the lives of employees. Ultimately, this will improve the success of a business while allowing a ripple effect at familial and societal levels. All those involved will benefit.

I see a huge opportunity to create a global Human Skills Institute here in West Donegal, which will be a place where the design and delivery of modules of learning are informed by world-class research. In 2024, I registered the Human Skills Institute as a limited company. I'm encouraged by how important a role human skills will play in the workplace of the future, a future that's already here. I'm also satisfied that this Human Skills Institute has found a natural home as well as an increasing need for its emergence. This book is part of that vision.

About this book

This book is not an academic one. Although it's important to dip into the academic world and reference current research, these chapters are mostly based on my experiences of working with businesses and my observations of people closer to home who have left a lasting impression on me.

My own personal journey has been fundamental, too. A big part of my life has been circled by three life-changing illnesses: alcoholism, heart disease and depression. I try not to hide behind any of them, so this book includes me but is not about me. Each of these potentially fatal illnesses and the subsequent recovery from each has heightened my gratitude for many things as well as my desire to help others who suffer one of these conditions or similar.

When initially asked about the book's primary audience, I had to move away from the lazy answer of 'everyone'. I would like the book to benefit anyone who has a role or responsibility in leadership, management, workplace learning, human resources, learning and development, coaching, sport, education and community building. I believe there are benefits in developing a greater understanding of human skills as well as improving the methodology of reaching the learner at scale.

You'll find three distinct sections in each chapter, starting with an explanation of a specific human skill and my experience of it. The 'Closer to home' section draws on inspiration from someone I know and have been impressed by, or a story from my community in Donegal. Finally, 'Musings from Madonna's Caravan' provides a reflective end to each chapter. This is a compact caravan that my wife, Toni, and I bought after I went through a heart event in 2018, in the hope that it would help me to slow down and decrease my chances of ending up back in a hospital theatre. It took some time but Madonna's Caravan became the place where I went to read and reflect. By this virtue it became the natural location for the writing of much of this book. Equally, the town of Cala de Mijas in Spain and an apartment there overlooking the sea provided an inspirational environment for perhaps 40 per cent of the writing. It holds an important place in my heart and soul.

The tone and style of the book is informal and conversational. My hope is that it's inspirational. It would be great to believe that all the research and data I've gathered can be used in your life as well as passed on to others in a way that makes a difference. The book has been written in such a way that you can.

It's important to note here that MIT's research, which was conducted by the Jameel World Education Lab, led to the creation of a Human Skills Matrix featuring 24 durable skills that workers need to thrive in today's rapidly evolving organisations. Some of the 20 skills I've written about in this book feature in MIT's Matrix; others are skills I've included as they are consistently mentioned in classroom and workplace learning settings. However, each human skill is important in its own way, and all of them are learnable.

Chapter 1

Connecting through storytelling

Storytelling is a timeless and universal craft that spans cultures, eras and now, social media. It's the art of conveying events, experiences or messages through words, images, sounds or actions. Storytelling is important in business sales and customer service for several reasons. It can enhance the customer experience, build trust and foster stronger connections between a brand, a company and its customers. For that reason and many more, it's an essential human skill.

My uncle and godfather, Murray Boyle, was a storyteller. I didn't know it at the time and neither did he, but to me, as a child living in New Jersey, USA, he always seemed to be telling stories. At that time, I had yet to set foot in Ireland but Murray would tell stories about Tory Island, off the coast of Donegal, and the characters who lived there, in a way that gave me a connection to the county I would later call home. I was to learn later in life that Murray himself had never been to Tory Island but that never restricted his imagination or the content of his stories. My father, Murray's brother, would listen to Murray's stories but not with the same enthusiasm that I would. 'He can never tell the same story twice and adds on parts that weren't there before,' my father would observe. This didn't really matter to me – if the story was good and caught my imagination, an occasional add-on simply provided flavour.

The Irish are widely regarded to be exceptional storytellers, a reputation grounded in a rich cultural history and a strong oral tradition. The Irish are known for their humour, wit and ability to find the extraordinary in the ordinary, making their stories engaging and entertaining. In hindsight, this is what Uncle Murray was doing. He was taking ordinary stories from people he'd worked with in Scotland, who were from Tory Island, yet creating extraordinary stories laced with imaginary characters, some human and some mythical sea monsters, and combining all these elements in a very graphic way. He'd laugh out loud when he'd tell us the punchline or the key part of the story, and others laughed at his laughter as much as at the story. To me, it was theatre.

Storytelling has been used in business for thousands of years. Traders and merchants used stories to share information about products, trade routes and markets. These merchants became great storytellers, and this became a key part of their success. From the 1950s onwards, TV and magazine advertising navigated its way through new ways of selling products and services, and again the form of storytelling changed – but the need for it didn't.

In more recent years, the evolution of the digital world has seen even more change and at a more rapid pace. Would the use of social media and other platforms that allow businesses to trade see an end to the practice of storytelling? The answer is no. Storytelling and the power of stories to connect with people on an emotional level is very much part of the social media sales toolkit. At their core, Instagram, Facebook, Snapchat and TikTok are storytelling platforms. The principles of storytelling remain the same, but where we tell stories has changed.

There's a need to equip people with the timeless art and skill of storytelling to ensure that connection is still created with a human touch and enhanced but not replaced by technology. Today, storytelling takes on the form of interactive media. Thanks to advancements in technology, we're not just exploring stories from history or science – we're also discovering each other's tales. From students and journalists to cooks and photographers, we've become the new breed of digital storytellers.

Closer to home

Although my Uncle Murray was my first introduction to storytelling, when I moved to Ireland at the age of eight, I stepped onto an island of storytellers. One of my early schoolteachers, my namesake, was a master storyteller. His passions – sport, Irish politics, nature and the outdoors – fuelled the continuous stream of stories he told. These stories were vivid, real and believable, often featuring characters from our local area. Although I tried to play the cool, 'I have no interest in education' person, I was fascinated by all of Charlie Boyle's tales, which he regaled us with in a way that brought the characters vividly to life in the classroom. The stories were relatable and became his way of teaching, influencing all of the areas he referred to and making each of the subjects more interesting. I waited in anticipation for our history lessons, where he'd talk about local heroes who, in his eyes, were as worthy of mention as the national figures of the early 1970s.

I learned that the rich tradition of storytelling, in both the ancient myths and modern literature, was important. Fionn Mac Cumhaill and his son Oisin, James Joyce, W B Yeats, Oscar Wilde, Jonathan Swift and Peig Sayers were some of the characters and storytellers we heard about as schoolboys. Later, people like Roddy Doyle brought Irish life into book and screen form with some outstanding stories such as *The Commitments*. Seamus Heaney wrote poetry that had the ability to bring you right to the place and time he was describing. My favourite poem of all time is one by Heaney called 'Markings' (1991), where he describes lads out playing football in a field where the only official markings were four jackets as goalposts. The colour, reality and vividness in this poem bring those of us who played these games of football in those fields right back and into them in a way in which nothing else can. To me, the greatest line in this poem, or indeed of any poem I know, is 'There was fleetness, furtherance, untiredness, in time that was extra, unforeseen and free'.

These storytellers have contributed to Ireland's reputation as a land of rich narrative tradition, capturing the imagination of readers and listeners around the world. Yet, on reflection, there were storytellers all around us in our community in West Donegal. There were and still are many different types of storytellers locally, from those who hold and protect the integrity of stories handed down from generation to generation and are meticulous in their narration of insightful stories that we often only take an interest in as we get older. There are those who are perhaps at the other end of the storytelling arc who might be better known for telling a good yarn, sprinkled with imagination and humour yet unlikely to reach the threshold of literary integrity and rigour. But in their own way, we allow them the artistic licence to entertain us, and they do. Storytelling has room for all.

Commercially, storytelling has worked extremely effectively in selling products and services. I watched this play out in a positive way on Jools Holland's *Annual Hootenanny* show on New Year's Eve 2023. A young Donegal singer and guitar player called Muireann Bradley was an unexpected guest amid a line-up of globally famous singers and musicians – a talented 17-year-old who was being given a chance to shine on one of the most-watched TV programmes of the year. Jools is known for his knack of inviting fresh, up-and-coming talent onto his show to expose them to a wider audience and give them a chance to progress their career. Muireann was afforded the opportunity to not only sing but also tell her story.

She explained that, as a young girl, she'd sit in the back of her dad's car, where she'd listen to Appalachian-influenced music and a unique form of bluegrass that he was passionate about. She went on to describe accompanying her dad to venues and watching him set up his sound equipment and play to audiences from a few to many. In a humble and quiet manner, Muireann then explained that during the Covid-19 lockdown and with time on her side, she worked hard at her guitar playing, a key element of her performance. Her rendition of 'Candyman' by the Reverend Gary Davis, itself a great story, was outstanding. Rod Stewart, Joss Stone, Ruby Turner and others surrounded her with love and inclusion ensuring she took centre stage for the final song of the night – a tribute to her talent and her story.

If music is the product that Muireann Bradley is promoting as she embarks on a career in the industry, it's the story she tells that resonates strongly and has helped her career take off since that New Year's Eve performance on Jools Holland's show. People will buy the product, but making sure there's a story well told gives artists a great advantage in an industry that's difficult to crack. Millions heard both the story and the music that night, so when her UK and Irish tour was promoted in the months following her appearance, it was a major success. Customers love a good story and will pay to be part of it. The more personal the story, the more global its reach.

Musings from Madonna's Caravan

It's only been in recent years that I've become fully aware of the power of storytelling in business. I associated storytelling with literature and entertainment but not with the advantage it could provide to a business, organisation or brand. I would've given a lot more credit to the 5 Ps of product, placement, promotion, price and people as a basis for selling. In a business or organisation, sales are essential regardless of whether it's a for-profit or a not-for-profit enterprise.

In 2017, I attended a two-day sales seminar to see if there was anything fresh and innovative that could be added to the service provided by Customer Service Excellence Ireland. Day two was set aside for storytelling. My understanding of that in advance as well as my expectations were low. However, the day added greatly to my appreciation and understanding of the power of storytelling in business. If you're selling in the current economy, the product or service you're providing or proposing is most likely available elsewhere. Two major factors can differentiate you from others who are selling that same product or service. One is the overall customer experience, and the other is the compelling story that surrounds it.

Music has been a constant in my life. My favourites tend to be singers and bands who have produced meaningful songs about their era or the region they grew up in. The Squeeze song 'Labelled with Love' and Bruce Springsteen's 'My Hometown' both paint a clear and vivid picture in my head of what the writer wishes me to connect with emotionally. In his song 'Nothing But the Same Old Story', Paul Brady describes how someone feels they're being treated with suspicion and not being included. In his song 'Boys of Summer', Don Henley takes me back to my youth and those with whom I grew up, some of whom have passed to their eternal reward. These and many other songwriters are great storytellers who took us through our lives, but there's also scenery and imagination involved. It was and is the stories within these songs that attract me to them. I'm sold on the story.

I can't help but believe that storytelling is a human skill

that would add value to young students as well as to those in the workplace. It requires the ability to articulate and explain thoughts and engage an audience. Storytelling encourages creativity and imagination and allows for out of the box thinking and different perspectives. It can enhance understanding of different characters and therefore help to develop empathy and a deeper understanding of human emotions. Storytelling can be a powerful way to improve cultural awareness at a time when it's vitally needed. The ability and confidence to be able to construct and tell a story helps with public speaking, and this would be a great advantage in business as well as socially. Incorporating storytelling into the curriculum, either as a stand-alone subject or integrated into existing ones, could provide a well-rounded educational experience that equips students with essential life skills. This is also true for lifelong and work-based learning programmes. I believe that businesses and brands as well as individuals selling their products and services can further improve their ability to tell their story and by doing so create a stronger connection with the customers they serve.

Chapter 2
Community building and social impact

The ten elements of community building and social impact I outline below align with widely recognised principles in the field of community development and collaborative action. Community building and social impact are interconnected human skills that aim to create strong, inclusive and supportive groups while fostering positive change within society. The elements of importance include:

→ inclusion and diversity

→ collaboration and participation

→ empowerment and capacity building

→ sustainability and longevity

→ mutual support and social networks

→ accountability and transparency

→ adaptability and flexibility

→ shared resources and reciprocity

→ celebrating and recognising successes and achievements.

Together, these features create a foundation for meaningful community engagement and drive social impact that can lead to lasting positive change. Community leadership is a vital element of society as the impact that a community has on its citizens and vice versa forms the fabric of that society. The above list was derived from the work of academics and best practice experts. I enjoyed reading the reasons behind the list and then comparing them to something I witnessed in a local setting a few years ago.

Closer to home

Twenty years of my life have been spent outside of Ireland, living in the US and the UK. The other 40 years have been spent in West Donegal, where I feel lucky to have been immersed in and nurtured by my community. In my experience, the adage that it takes a village to raise a child is true. The saying emphasises that a child's upbringing is a communal effort involving many different people and groups who know the child, from parents and teachers to neighbours, youth leaders and football coaches. The idea underscores the wider belief that the collective involvement of a community is essential in achieving a certain goal or completing a task such as raising a child, but also much more. Essentially, it's a friendly reminder that asking for help with hard things is OK, because that's the way we've been designed. And, let's face it, many hands do make light work.

In 1970, at the age of eight, I arrived in Mullaghduff, a small townland in West Donegal, from New Jersey, where I was born. Both my parents were from the local area as well as at least three generations that we can trace back. Here I became aware of a community that included many cousins and family friends. I spent as much, if not more, time in the houses of relatives and neighbours as I did in my own house. We seemed to play football for hours in many different fields with games varying from three of us playing 'three and in' to larger ones of 20 youngsters, which often ended in dispute over whether a goal was over the line or not.

We played in the sea, often 'borrowing' boats from a local fibreglass factory and heading out to sea with up to 25 youngsters on board, none of whom was over the age of 14. A few times, the local parish priest would intervene under the instruction of a concerned parent or neighbour. We'd get a telling off but in many ways that added to the risk and fun of it all. As a generation we were possibly not as mindful of the Church's standing as the generations before us, so I'm not sure what, if any, impact the priest's intervention had on our sailing aspirations. We were respectful as we listened to his ill-fated lecture, but as soon as he was up the road, we were back in the water.

When I wasn't playing on the field or in the sea, I found another source of community togetherness involving discipline and structure – the local marching band. We had two bands in our townland. The 'big band' was one of many fife and drum bands and its membership was made up completely of boys and men. We also had the 'wee band', which consisted of accordions, melodicas, tin whistles and drums. This was a band of local boys and girls, mostly between the ages of 10 and 18. Our townland of Mullaghduff, with a population of approximately 250 people, took its bands seriously. The competition between us and bands from neighbouring townlands was intense. At 11, I was asked to play the triangle in the wee band, and this was a huge act of inclusion in a community that I was neither born nor raised in. In hindsight, this started my official and proud journey as a member of the local community and I felt part of something important. I'm certainly not the only one to have benefited from the camaraderie and support of the institution during its existence.

Thirty years before my experience in the band, on 10 May 1943, a German mine floated into the nearby shoreline of Ballymanus. Young and older men from the area went to see what was involved and although they were warned not to go near the mine, a rope was tied around the device and the group pulled it towards the rocky shoreline. At 9.43 pm, as darkness was falling, the mine exploded, killing 19 young men aged between 13 and 34 in what was the second biggest loss of life in Ireland during the Second World War. It was a horrific scene. Bodies were thrown out to sea and back on the rocks, dismembered and recovered in many cases with only a limb remaining. The explosion was heard by people many miles away. My father, who was 14 at the time, was taking water home in buckets and the ground shook where he was, more than four miles away. My mother, then aged 13, was closer to Ballymanus and she too was doing household duties when the mine exploded. She'd been in the same classroom earlier that day as two of those who died. It was a traumatic event for the people of our area and the trauma has had an impact to this day.

A tragedy of comparable proportions took place in a small Donegal village in 2022, when ten people were killed in a suspected gas explosion at a convenience store in Creeslough. There are almost 80 years between the two events at Ballymanus and Creeslough, yet the support offered to the local communities affected in each and the transparency around establishing the truth of what happened differ greatly. In Creeslough, evidence was preserved and a police investigation, while not without its difficulties, commenced immediately. However, at the time of the Ballymanus explosion, while an inquest was held the day following the explosion, the local clergy and government politicians opposed the idea of holding a formal inquiry. The view was that any investigation would only serve to embarrass the local community, and families were instead instructed to let the matter rest and console themselves with prayer.

The distress and trauma that people felt because of the Ballymanus mine disaster, just like the explosion in Creeslough decades later, was profound and damaging. Although it happened during the Second World War, the west of Ireland wasn't directly impacted in terms of German bombings and nothing could have prepared the area for a tragedy of such immense proportions. Several of those who played in the Mullaghduff band were killed and the organisation subsequently acted as a positive distraction at a time of great need. Sport, including football, boxing and athletics, also played its part and again there were key and committed locals within the community who showed strength and leadership in ensuring that young and older men could participate in musical and sporting activities. Community effort became a critical factor for healing, albeit slowly. I was aware of the Ballymanus tragedy as a child and in my teenage years, but a silence or at best a dripfeed of information accompanied any mention of it.

My friends and I carried on playing and enjoying days out with the wee band until its final appearance in 1979 and a win at the then-famous Letterkenny Folk Festival. The big band experienced a period of transition in the years ahead that included a bid to attract younger members and females and also forced existing members to consider their commitment to the organisation. Many of the long-standing musicians were also fishermen who spent weeks at sea and while passionate about the band they were unable to commit to regular practice. Intervention from a music tutor from the north was the catalyst for change that everyone supported. David Foster from Ballyclare in County Antrim had the benefit of being an outside voice and as such he was able to outline the level of rigour, discipline and commitment that was required if the band was serious about winning an All-Ireland Fleadh Cheoil, a national competition and a dream of many. This proposal for change was risky and could easily have split opinion and divided the band. But, at a meeting to decide the future direction of the band, I watched a transformation that would result in a profound social impact on the townland of Mullaghduff.

Band members who couldn't give their full commitment (including me) stepped aside to leave room for new members. I was most impressed, however, by the response of the fishermen to the changes being sought. They looked forward to coming ashore for the important days and yet they could see a bigger picture and a longer-term gain for the group. Four years later, the new, young and energetic band won its first All-Ireland in 1992. Directed by a Protestant from Ballycastle (at a time when Ireland was in the depths of the Troubles and sectarian division) and comprising both male and female members in the marching drill (a key element of the competition created by local man Seamus Gallagher), the band was an inspiring example of diversity. Winning the competition was a truly sensational day for Mullaghduff and the surrounding area. The band would go on to win a further 13 All-Ireland titles.

The victories were sweet, but it was in the transformation of the band, the journey and development of competent, confident children into adolescents and well-rounded adults that the real victory lay. Was this a factor in healing from the Ballymanus tragedy? In many ways, absolutely. Here was a once-damaged and silenced townland, now confident yet humbled in its achievements at national level. The area had found its voice through its music. It's said that you'll never be successful if you have the mentality of a victim, and this played out as the band represented all of us in finding our place on a national stage. The objective of winning was not to resolve trauma, but it certainly played a big part in that.

The success of the band had a ripple effect on others, too. The youth believed in their abilities and were confident without swagger. They made decisions about progressing to university or applying for work positions that previously would've felt beyond them. During these All-Ireland band wins, in the mid-1990s, the townland of Mullaghduff won a national Tidy Towns award. It was another example of hard work and commitment by those involved but it also had elements of the theory often applied to economics that a rising tide lifts all boats. The confidence and uplift being played out within the band community reverberated throughout the whole community. The positive social impact of these achievements was evident then and remains so today. Those who've gone through similar changes will identify with the process and be able to reflect on the far-reaching impact that community success can have.

Musings from Madonna's Caravan

When you look around, you can see that success leaves clues. As a young man in West Donegal, lessons in community building and social impact were under my nose, and my experience of the band is one that's stayed with me as an important example of success. I knew each of the characters and had enough exposure of being a former member to understand the difficulties around the commitment required for transformational change, but also the need for it. I wasn't always directly involved but had a ringside seat to the events that brought about the change. What I've learned over the years is that, below the surface of community-led success, there's often a dark and, at times, ugly underbelly of tension, resentment and disagreement. Conflict is an inevitable element of growth. Egos emerge, communication can be challenging and people can feel left out. Some will dominate while others isolate, and it takes a strong vision and often unpopular leadership to navigate through change and towards success.

At the end of this chapter, you may wish to return to the beginning and re-read the ten features listed at the start. When examining community success, leadership doesn't always mean the obvious front person, as important as they are. It could be the quiet voice in the corner suggesting that they could step down for the greater good, sacrificing their pleasure for a longer-term social gain. It takes a village not only to raise a child but to build and maintain a community that can achieve positive social impact.

Chapter 3

Psychological safety

Psychological safety is critically important in various contexts, including workplaces, schools, teams and communities. I've lived in them all. A psychologically safe environment is one in which individuals feel safe to express themselves, take risks, share ideas and voice concerns without fear of embarrassment, rejection, ridicule or punishment. It's also a human skill simply because humans are involved in the environment. At a time when innovation and change are constant, in many ways we're navigating change without a roadmap. Collaboration has never been so important. When people feel psychologically safe, they're more likely to share creative ideas and raise concerns, leading to innovation and problem solving. Diverse perspectives contribute to better decisions, but these can only surface in an environment in which individuals feel secure.

Psychological safety fosters trust and inclusion, leading to higher morale and a deeper connection to the organisation. Employees who feel heard and valued are less likely to leave their jobs and, at a time when recruitment and retention are big challenges, retaining good team members is vital. This is the same in a community or indeed a family setting. People need to have a voice and if the environment doesn't allow for all voices to be heard, then there's a problem. Teamwork and collaboration require psychological safety. Many of you will have worked in, or been part of, organisations where you may not have felt comfortable bringing something to the attention of management, as you knew it just wouldn't land well. You must also accept that at some stage of your life, you were the cause of the unsafe place because you were too caught up in your own agenda. Few people go through life without being both the cause and the victim of poor psychological safety. A reflection from my own life is that I've seen where I've shut down the thoughts and opinions of others and that was a failing. However, if this experience informs my current efforts to support those who wish to create a good workplace or community culture, I see that as making amends.

Closer to home

My townland of Mullaghduff in West Donegal is, like many in Ireland, a place of scenic beauty and generations of great characters. The adjoining areas of the Rosses and Gaoth Dobhair are the same. In 1978, I was 15 and weaving into the local happenings, discos in the local youth club, marching bands, watching *Top of the Pops*, all while in my second year at secondary school in Falcarragh, about 40 minutes away by bus. Having been a boarding student in the first year and not taking to the regime of life in a dormitory, I felt unsettled and maybe in hindsight struggled with identity and sense of place. But it was nothing major and in the big scheme of things nowhere near what others were going through.

That summer, I was playing soccer for an under 16s team from our townland. A local and significant adult, Eugene Greene, had taken time out of his life to treat us with respect and care. He invested the most important thing an adult can offer: his time. Along with it, he added a competitive spirit, and there was a league and championship competition of clubs from the Gaeltacht area of West Donegal. Because we had a small catchment area, Eugene drafted in a few players from neighbouring townlands and by giving us a safe environment and a non-judgemental atmosphere, we thrived as a team. It wasn't the English First Division but the lesson was there nonetheless. There's a well-known Gaeilge saying, *'Mol an Óige, agus tiocfidh sí'*, which translates as 'Praise the young and they will flourish.' We made the final and were beaten on penalties but the victory was in the climb, the journey, the togetherness, the fun, the fights, the commitment. Looking back, this was psychological safety in action, and Eugene created this safe place for learning, playing, making mistakes and accountability. He's still doing it today, almost 50 years later, but with upholstery and art classes at a community project he runs really well with the same simple strategy of making a safe place available for others to flourish. In this example, it's for people of all ages.

Shortly after this football final in 1978, as I contemplated another year at school in Falcarragh, Paddy Murray O'Donnell, a teacher at the local Rosses Community

School, asked me if I'd consider joining his secondary school. It was nearer to where I lived and reopening in a new building in Dungloe, six miles away. He also threw in that he'd make me captain of the senior soccer team. Paddy Murray was already someone I knew and trusted. I'd been in his presence with the local marching band and around the hall, and he was always hugely encouraging in a nice and level way. I'd made my decision that I'd go to this new school and all that remained to be done was the breaking of the news to my mother and father.

Paddy Murray is the best example I've ever encountered of a leader who values psychological safety, and once again the experience was at home, under my feet. In his role as sports master, history and English teacher at the secondary school, which by this time I'd moved to and felt at home in from the first hour, Paddy was a central figure in the lives of many. He seldom criticised unless it was really necessary and tended to 'catch you in' as opposed to others who delighted in catching you out. Devoid of an overinflated ego but full of the local pride he created around any project, team or marching band, Paddy was a leader of the highest ilk. I often felt that his teaching of history and English was minimal in comparison to his performance as the football manager of various school teams. However, because we were protective of his efforts for us, we dug deep to get the marks required to make it look as if he was equal to Aristotle.

Paddy had been involved in the success of Packie Bonner, who'd later go on to be the Glasgow Celtic and Ireland goalkeeper, and at one point in his career was mentioned as one of the world's best keepers. Packie often recognised Paddy's contribution. Likewise, the singer Daniel O'Donnell, who's maintained a streak of having at least one album in the UK top 40 every year for more than 33 years, was also a pupil of Paddy's. No musician or band has enjoyed similar success and Daniel has also acknowledged Paddy's encouragement and presence as sources of safety that contributed to his world-class career.

Paddy nurtured anyone he encountered, whether it was in a classroom or the sports hall. He managed football teams to All-Ireland success and was involved with his Mullaghduff Fife and Drum band, which would go on to dominate at All-Ireland level as well. Paddy was a compassionate leader. He created psychologically safe places whether it was in the history class, on the field or the local hall at band practice. He had an 'it'll work out all right' type of attitude but with a vision to believe in better things.

I remember on one occasion, 16-year-old Bernard Greene was sitting beside me in one of Paddy's classes. As was normal, halfway through the class, Paddy told us to 'revise what we did last week', when one of the cheeky Dungloe lads said, 'But we didn't do anything last week, Sir,' to which Paddy replied, 'Revise it anyway,' as he left the class. He had more important matters to contend with, such as putting up a team sheet on the sports board or ringing a school in Letterkenny to arrange a venue for a match. Bernard wasn't into football and had even less interest in history. I could see him putting a few pens and maybe even a book into his bag, and he said softly, 'F*** this, Charlie, I'm away.' I watched him leave through the window and that was the last I saw of him for 40 years.

I liked Bernard but could see that school wasn't for him. Football and history weren't his forte either, but Paddy didn't exclude him. As the class ended and I was passing Paddy at the door, I thought I should tell him that we were down a trooper and it was unlikely he would return. Paddy smiled and said, 'Do you know something, he'll be all right.' Paddy was right. Bernard enrolled in a local carpentry course, later moving to London where he went on to employ many staff, installing windows. Go figure! He has since moved back home and commutes to London to look after his successful business.

I also witnessed Paddy's kindness to those we might today call the marginalised. He'd give them his time and a chat. He didn't overdo anything but was the person I continue to think of when company culture or a psychologically safe place to work is mentioned. Paddy's proudest day was in 1995, when he was elected Mayor of Mullaghduff. The election, a charity fundraiser, was fought with an intensity that would put a US election to shame. Paddy beat another local hero, Michael Rodgers, in the count, which resulted in Paddy's cavalcade being re-routed as Michael and his supporters blocked Paddy's intended celebratory route. Paddy held onto the chain of office for a record only matched by the great Clint Eastwood as Mayor of Carmel in California. His campaign team, namely his loyal and trusted wife Moya, refused to allow another election and even today the chain remains in Paddy's house, renamed Gracie Mansion.

Paddy died in 2014, leaving us richer for his presence in another place of psychological safety. He remains our forever mayor and an example of a good person. His father, Murray O'Donnell, was our favourite shopkeeper in the area. I first met Murray when he was in his seventies and his welcome was the same for a then impressionable eight-year-old, arriving from America, as it was for any of his adult customers. Murray never judged or criticised. He encouraged and praised. This would, of course, have helped his business as in those days, mothers would send their children to the local shops to buy the groceries and it would be 'written in the book', the credit card of its time. The children doing the shopping would've liked Murray and therefore, most of them chose to frequent his shop. Murray had two shop girls, sisters Annie and Sophie Boyle. Both had worked in Murray's shop for years, and Annie lived in the O'Donnell family household.

It felt safe being in Murray's shop. Annie or Sophie would get the groceries from behind the counter and, as you waited, Murray would come in from the adjoining house to talk. He'd ask what was going on in terms of football, the marching band up the road or school, and had a genuine interest in you as a person. His level of encouragement was, in hindsight, a significant factor in a townland that had suffered a major trauma in the shape of the Ballymanus mine disaster. Murray was in many ways a counsellor – a trusted, steady and gentle person. He was much more than a shopkeeper. It was said that his father was the first to bring tea into West Donegal and that Murray was the last to sell paraffin, used for lamps. He sold bacon but also coffins. This innovation and product range made this tiny shop a treasure but it was the psychological safety we experienced at Murray's that was perhaps his most unique selling point.

Musings from Madonna's Caravan

Culture in a workplace, community, school or team is as important as the structure and strategy employed. It's as important as the products or services being delivered, the lesson being taught, and is the platform on which the success or failure of a project depends. The fear of failure or ridicule silences innovative ideas.

I've learned much, as have many of my friends and contemporaries, from the examples of people such as Paddy Murray O'Donnell and his father, Murray. In the economy and society in which we now find ourselves, the requirement for psychological safety is of vital importance. Psychological safety doesn't represent an undisciplined free for all. It's not a formal academic discipline but a growing field of study and practice within organisational psychology, leadership and workplace culture. It's a positive trend that shows that businesses are increasingly looking at their internal customer and workplace experience. The customer experience and hence sales or other outcomes are merely a reflection of the culture of the organisation. Psychological safety is central to this and therefore is a human skill of significant importance.

The fact that I was blessed with three local examples of people who embody the skill of psychological safety is not lost on me. The townland and beyond benefited from their presence immensely. Thank you, Paddy and Murray.

Chapter 4

Leadership

Reflecting on leadership as a human skill, my mind immediately goes back to my childhood. In the early 1970s, Owenie 'Charlie' Boyle owned a field in Bunaman near Annagry in West Donegal. (Although we shared the same name, we weren't related and Owenie was a family friend.) Like many fields in the area, it was bumpy and rough, with rushes growing in big chunks, spotted throughout the field. It was right beside Murlough lake, and for those in the surrounding townlands, this was the 'field of dreams' where, on many evenings, a group of up to 20 young and indeed older lads and men would gather to play soccer.

I was around ten years old and too young to play, but not too young to take it all in. James Gildea, who was probably in his twenties at the time, was what I now know to be a leader. Through the channels of communication that worked for us back then, the group would show up, teams would be picked, jumpers placed on the ground or sticks would act as goalposts. James would have been central to all of this yet he didn't make a big fuss or noise. He had an agreeable manner at a time when, believe me, agreeableness was not a default setting for many of the players! Fellas who were quiet and shy could go into an alter ego once the ball was introduced and get all worked up and aggressive, while others used the opportunity to express their extraordinary ball skills as they weaved majestically around much bigger and bulkier men while keeping the ball away from the rushes, which acted like an extra defender.

The rules were simple. There were none, or at most they were made up as the game progressed. If somebody claimed the ball had crossed a line, the VAR (video assistant referee) of the time was 'Shut up your mouth'. So, unless the ball went through the posts and into the lake, it wasn't a goal. Games were played until the light died. The appetite was such that even a team that were maybe five goals ahead would agree to the unwritten and well-established 'last goal the winner', giving every chance to the underdogs to claim victory from the jaws of darkness and dispute. Again, Seamus Heaney captures the magic of these games in his poem 'Markings' when he reminds us 'there was furtherance, untiredness and fleetness'.

Even though I didn't or couldn't name it at the time, James Gildea was a compassionate leader. To us younger ones, he was 'sound'. He would say, 'Yous can help to get the ball out of the lake tonight lads or be ball boys.' He'd take time to point to where he wanted us to be, all with a straight face. This was a huge thing and, like whippets, we'd recover the ball from the 'whin bushes' (or *fhun* bushes if you were from down Mullaghduff way) when the ball went into them, throw it out quickly so the game could proceed, and then maybe take ten minutes to get back out, covered in stabs and needles from the bushes. Even though the odd lad or two would never say anything much, you'd hear James saying, 'Ah, fair play to you, that's great work.' I couldn't wait until someone kicked the ball out of play (usually one of the Annagry men). It was like rocket fuel.

This was an apprenticeship, a development squad. The learning was real and raw but highly engaging and entertaining. I felt part of something. I quietly observed the different characters. Technology was completely absent. It was safe, exhausting, fast, but as people went off in different directions after the game, I tried to find out when they'd be back again so I could return to retrieve the ball more quickly and smartly. On the surface, this was all simple stuff but it reached a deeper level in the way that it connected people, and reflecting back to that time I can see that it required leadership of a certain kind to work. The field was always full in the summer months. Success leaves clues.

I've always been interested in the ability of people to lead and influence. As a young boy growing up in Donegal, I didn't realise James Gildea was in fact a brilliant leader, as my view of the archetypal leader was largely shaped by those who had been involved in wars and politics during the 20th century. Charismatic leaders such as Winston Churchill, Franklin D Roosevelt and later John F Kennedy became icons through their ability to mobilise the masses, as was required at the time. There were, of course, domineering and totalitarian leaders such as Adolf Hitler and Joseph Stalin yet also democratic leaders such as Mahatma Gandhi, who favoured a pacifist approach based on consensus.

In Ireland, history and politics were dominated by the Irish civil war in the 1920s and the Troubles in Northern Ireland from the early 1970s onwards and, as a result, Michael Collins, Eamon de Valera and later, John Hume, Ian Paisley and others dominated my image of leadership. Some of these leaders I respected and others I feared.

As we hit the 25 per cent mark of the 21st century, leadership has become an ever-changing and complex construct. Balancing the expectations and interests of various stakeholders, including employees, customers, investors and the community, has become increasingly ambiguous. The integration of AI and automation in various industries demands leaders who can understand and leverage these technologies effectively. Constant innovation in digital tools and platforms requires leaders to be tech savvy and open to change at alarming rates.

Leading a diverse, neurodivergent, multicultural workforce necessitates sensitivity and adaptability to different cultural norms and practices. There's also a growing emphasis on sustainable practices and corporate social responsibility. Social impact is now a currency, and leaders must balance profit with ethical considerations or risk alienating a more discerning customer base who tend to seek out the story behind the business they're engaging with. Leaders must be willing to admit what they don't know and consult with and listen to those who do.

Attracting and retaining top talent in a constantly evolving competitive market is challenging, requiring innovative strategies in employee engagement and development. The Covid-19 pandemic disrupted the traditional office and workplace arrangement and hybrid working practices and working remotely have created fresh challenges in managing a dispersed workforce. Leadership is required to change how the place of work fits for the employee.

I've been fortunate and indeed privileged to have been involved in many projects from 1998–2024, during which time I've witnessed many different leadership styles – good, not so good and indifferent. After acquiring a master's in leadership and innovation at 55 years of age, I was finally able to combine the experience I was going through with academic theories based on strong and trusted research.

Leadership is often a gift that people have from birth yet it can also be learned and practised. Trends change and leaders often have to adapt quickly while, at other times, leaders create the change by disrupting the status quo. The glorification of the 60–70 hour week must end, along with standing on the sidelines at our children's sports fields replying to non-urgent emails on our mobile phones, so that we can be present for the moments that matter most.

Leadership is moving more towards servant leadership, where the hierarchical model is collapsing and the role of the leader is to help or serve other leaders in the team or organisation. The expectation and indeed demand is for a more considerate and compassionate type of leadership and one that helps everyone navigate the turbulent and unpredictable world we're living in. Impactful leadership can be both strong and compassionate.

As a model for this type of leadership, we can look back to the Tony Blair/Bill Clinton administrations that joined with others to bring about a solution to the Northern Ireland conflict, which many tried but failed to do in the past. While not without its challenges, the Good Friday Agreement was an example of a consensus approach that would not have been possible in the previous 10 or 20 years. For me and many generations in Ireland, both older and younger, this was a massive and highly significant event in our lives. I remember sitting up through the night in a flat in Canterbury, Kent, in April 1998, alone and tearful when news broke that there was an agreement and hence the hope of a lasting peace.

I'm attracted more and more to what we might now call compassionate leadership. By this I don't mean an over-compassionate approach in an organisation that doesn't have a sustainable profit model in place and weak and uncommitted staff are allowed to dictate the pace and performance. Instead, I'm talking about an organisation or business that has a clear and compelling vision and social impact. That social impact may be the creation of jobs in a rural area where the population has been in decline, or one that promotes women in equal proportion to their male colleagues. It could also be allowing workers to choose the hours that fit around their personal lives, within reason and balance. It encourages psychological safety so that innovation can thrive and mistakes aren't punished. (For more on psychological safety, see Chapter 3.) Some of us, like my childhood football coach James Gildea, have a natural ability to lead with compassion. By choosing balance and a desire to 'catch people in' as opposed to trying to catch people out, we can all develop the skill.

Closer to home

In the daylight hours of 6 December 1940 and later during a night of some of the worst sea storm conditions witnessed in West Donegal, a Dutch cargo ship, the *Stolwijk*, which was bringing supplies from Newfoundland to Liverpool as part of a convoy, ran into difficulties and went aground between the Donegal Islands and the mainland, near the island of Inisboffin. The ship's lifeboat was swept away, with some of the crew lost and a British Navy boat nearby tried hard but failed in its attempt to rescue the remaining crew in what were now hurricane-force conditions. The fate of the 18 remaining sailors was in peril and only a miracle or a very unlikely rescue would save their lives. Their boat, already having suffered damage, was likely to founder on the rocks of the unforgiving Donegal shoreline, and in the words of the song written by my good friend Jerry Early, 'the chances of survival on a night that were few'.

Too often we use the term 'beyond the call of duty' but this was a justified description of what happened next. These volunteer lifeboatmen were paid £2 for a callout. Although a decent sum in those war years, money wasn't a motivating factor. As they set off in the early hours of that December morning, there were seasoned fishermen, neighbours and family watching the single-engine boat head out on what one experienced island fisherman called a suicide rescue. Even in the depths of great danger, humour is important, and it was often said that the weather was so bad that even the married men kissed their wives as they left their homes that day!

On the neighbouring island of Owey, the head of the primary school, having heard about the lifeboat rescue, brought all the schoolchildren to the top of a hill to watch this boat of brave rescuers head out on a mission to save the lives of people they didn't know. Within the head's mind was the thought that this was history in the making, yet what kind of history was uncertain, as he led his pupils to and from their vantage point.

Each of the Arranmore lifeboat crew who sailed out brought different skills to the team dynamic: mechanical, navigational, calmness, strength, experience and so on. Here were men prepared to lay down their lives to carry out a rescue operation that could help other human beings off a boat that was certain to sink. This was compassion and courage at the ultimate level, with leadership as a vital requirement.

All 18 Dutch sailors on board the stricken *Stolwijk* were saved and brought to the safety of harbour. This was humanity at its finest. As well as compassionate leadership, it was a demonstration of collaborative leadership, emphasising teamwork, shared decision making and the importance of diverse perspectives. Collaborative leaders create environments in which all team members feel valued and empowered to contribute in a psychologically safe place where each voice can be heard. This was exhibited on the Arranmore lifeboat on 7 December 1940.

Musings from Madonna's Caravan

The story of the *Stolwijk* is one that I'm ashamed to say I only heard for the first time in 2019. I was nearly paralysed on the gravel road of Arranmore Island as Jerry Early, a native of the island and a former lifeboat member himself, told me the story, which was highly personal to him. His father Andrew would've witnessed the lifeboat going out on the morning of the rescue, and Jack Boyle, the lifeboat captain, was a lifelong friend. Andrew was still alive and Jerry and a friend had penned a song that profoundly represented the night of the rescue. I clearly remember standing in a group of around six others as Jerry stood overlooking the sea where the lifeboat would've sailed out and told our small but totally engaged group this epic and mostly understated story of compassionate leadership and humanity. I knew that this was a story that had to be told as it probably contains everything you need to know about leadership.

I've always admired great leadership when I've witnessed it or experienced its impact. My boyhood heroes were sporting leaders like Jock Stein, who led Celtic FC to a pinnacle of European success in 1967 with a team of players who came from within a 30-mile radius of Glasgow; or political leaders such as John Hume, who championed peace in Northern Ireland through non-violent means and against many odds. Later, my heroes became more localised and personal. Tony Doherty, a quiet, unassuming man, was a founding member of our local Gaelic Athletic Association (GAA) club Naomh Muire. Tony had a compelling vision to create a club that would cater for the need to express our youthful sporting energy in a way that acknowledged our Gaelic heritage and culture. When the rest of us wavered, his vision kept the club on a steady track of growth and strength to the position of pride it occupies today. As the club often developed and nurtured local talent, Tony watched many emigrate, robbing the team of its talent, yet he never saw this as a negative and would only look at what could be done in a positive manner.

As I've mentioned previously, in 2016, I was accepted to study for a master's in innovation and leadership, without the possession of a third-level degree. The system of 'recognition of prior learning and experience' is a welcome entry to university education with consideration given to experience and competency as opposed to the single measurement of qualification, as it allows so-called rough diamonds into the system. For me, the study was in many ways a life-changing process. I could see that leadership wasn't only about the John F Kennedys and Nelson Mandelas, as impressive as they were. It's also about ordinary people like Tony Doherty and his compassionate ability to give of his time and passion freely, and by doing so passing on his vision to a new generation. It's about the decision, following careful consideration, of Jack Boyle and his lifeboat crew on 7 December 1940, to rescue men who would otherwise have perished on the rocks of their Atlantic Ocean area of responsibility. Through the scope of academic study, these local leaders stood in front of me with a clarity that I can often fail to articulate. The experience of study enriched my love of my local area in a manner that inspired me to do more to highlight the greatness of what many would call simple people, yet now knowing we were standing in the presence of giants. The modern pathway of leadership is reflected in the leaders local to me. This reflection is powerful for me personally, but even more important, I believe, is to ensure that their stories are told and their leadership style and inspiration are used in a powerful and dynamic way to help the communities that they clearly loved. We must change the style of leadership to reflect 21st-century needs while not forgetting that the key components of leadership can be found in examples from the past.

Chapter 5

Accountability

Last year, I worked with a group of CEOs from five credit unions in Ireland. We created a list of human skills, which would later be delivered to their staff and management as an improved member experience programme. The plan was to focus on eight key human skills from an overall list of 24. Initially, only one of the CEOs chose accountability as a skill that should be included in the programme. His argument for its inclusion was quite compelling and over the course of several meetings he convinced all the other CEOs of the workplace requirement for accountability.

Two months later, I was in a room with clinical managers and senior administrators at the Mater Public Hospital in Dublin. Once again, they were working off a menu of 24 human skills as the framework for a patient experience programme that my company was tasked with delivering in partnership with the management and administrative teams at Ireland's busiest hospital. Based on the arguments raised in the credit union discussion, I outlined the case for accountability. I needn't have bothered, because all ten of the senior Mater team agreed on accountability as a key human skill and one that they wanted to be included in the upcoming training and development programme.

Helped by the credit union and Mater Hospital experiences, as a business, we researched accountability not only in the context of work. This allowed us to design training to fit with each of these sectors but also to develop a greater understanding of it. Accountability is crucial for several reasons, in personal, professional and societal contexts:

→ **Trust and credibility:** when people or organisations are accountable, they build trust. Accountability means taking responsibility for actions and outcomes, which fosters credibility. Trust is fundamental in relationships, workplaces and communities, and accountability helps to maintain it.

→ **Ownership and responsibility:** being accountable encourages individuals to take ownership of their actions. When people know they're responsible for the outcomes of their work or decisions, they tend to be more careful, thorough and proactive.

→ **Improvement and learning:** accountability provides opportunities for learning and growth. When individuals or organisations acknowledge mistakes or failures, they can identify areas for improvement and work on solutions. It promotes a culture of continuous development.

→ **Efficiency and performance:** in organisations, accountability drives performance. When employees are held accountable, they're more likely to meet goals and deadlines. It ensures that tasks are completed and responsibilities fulfilled, leading to higher productivity.

→ **Transparency and fairness:** accountability promotes transparency, making processes and decisions clear. It ensures that everyone understands their roles and responsibilities and actions are taken based on facts and fairness, reducing conflicts and fostering a sense of justice.

→ **Ethical behaviour:** accountability helps to prevent unethical behaviour. When individuals know they'll be held responsible for their actions, they're less likely to engage in misconduct. It enforces moral and ethical standards.

→ **Achievement of goals:** whether in business, personal life or public governance, accountability ensures that goals are pursued actively. It helps to track progress and ensures that commitments are honoured, making it easier to achieve desired outcomes.

Overall, accountability drives integrity, efficiency and progress, making it essential for building successful relationships, businesses and better societies. But its absence can result in terrible consequences.

The UK's Post Office scandal is one of the most significant miscarriages of justice in British legal history. It involved the wrongful conviction of hundreds of sub-postmasters for theft, fraud and false accounting due to flaws in the Post Office's Horizon IT system, developed by ICL/Fujitsu, which was introduced by the Post Office in 1999. The system was used for accounting and transactions at thousands of Post Office branches, but bugs in the system led to apparent discrepancies in branch accounts. Between 2000 and 2014, more than 700 sub-postmasters were prosecuted by the Post Office for alleged financial discrepancies. The Post Office insisted the Horizon system was robust and any shortfalls must have been due to theft or fraud. As a result, many sub-postmasters were convicted, fined and even imprisoned. Others were forced to repay large sums of money, lost their businesses or went bankrupt.

For years, and despite mounting evidence, the Post Office refused to accept that the Horizon system was flawed. It aggressively pursued legal action against sub-postmasters, often without considering alternative explanations for the discrepancies. The organisation failed to disclose crucial evidence about the system's known issues in court, and there were allegations of a cover-up by both the Post Office and Fujitsu. Many of those affected experienced devastating consequences. While some were imprisoned, others lost their homes, livelihoods and reputations. The emotional toll was severe, with some individuals suffering mental health problems and, in a few tragic cases, people committing suicide as a result of the stress and stigma. How painful and damaging this must have been.

This was a human tragedy that came about because of a lack of accountability early on in the saga. Sub-postmasters, led by a group action, sued the Post Office in a series of lawsuits. In 2019, the High Court ruled that the Horizon system was not reliable and that the Post Office had been wrong in its aggressive pursuit of legal action against sub-postmasters. The court found that the Post Office had acted in an 'oppressive' manner.

After the 2019 judgement, the Post Office agreed to pay £58 million in compensation to the group of 555 claimants, although much of this sum was consumed by legal costs. The British government and the Post Office have since faced growing pressure to fully compensate all victims, with additional compensation schemes being launched. There were calls for further investigations into Fujitsu, the company that developed the Horizon system, due to its role in providing flawed evidence and testimony during the trials. At the time of writing, legal battles and the search for justice for all those affected continue.

The scandal highlighted deep institutional failures within the Post Office, which had acted as both investigator and prosecutor in the cases against the sub-postmasters. It also raised questions about corporate governance, accountability and how public institutions handle failures and their impact on individuals. The huge damage done to the Post Office, once an iconic and trusted UK brand, as well as to the many who suffered because of false accusations of fraud, had its origins in poor accountability.

Closer to home

I was raised Catholic. This wasn't my choice but you're either born into a faith of some kind or none. I went through the normal Catholic rituals of baptism, first communion, confirmation and marriage. I went through divorce as well, but the Church doesn't trade in that, so that's another story. I went through a Catholic education in the 1970s and early 1980s. The Church and the local parish priest had a strong influence locally. In hindsight, even at a young age, I found many priests to be shallow and distant. Occasionally, I met one who was less coercive and controlling, but overall, I wasn't a big fan.

On a few occasions in our mid-teens, a close group of us would cross the line in terms of low-level anti-social behaviour such as the 'borrowing' of fibreglass items from a local factory and using them as boats as I mentioned earlier. On another occasion we attempted, through our idea of a séance, to bring Elvis back from the dead a year after he checked out. Both incidents landed at the feet of the local priest, who came to read us his version of the Riot Act and warned us that he didn't want to hear any more 'carry on'. We just got better at hiding the 'carry on', so he heard no more. Did we respect his warning? I'm not sure that we did. We tended to take guidance and direction and the odd earful from other community figures, mostly those involved in sports or youth clubs, whom we respected. We were aware that we didn't have the same fear of the Church and its clergy as our parents did, or at least the group I was around didn't seem to.

Several years later, we'd be faced with the facts of widespread abuse of children within the Irish Catholic Church. The scandal in Ireland, involving both the Catholic Church and state-run institutions, is one of the most significant cases of systemic abuse and cover-up in modern history. It involved decades of sexual, physical and emotional abuse of children by priests, religious clergy and staff at institutions run by the Catholic Church, often with the complicity of the state. The full extent of the abuse began to emerge publicly in the 1990s and 2000s, leading to a series of major inquiries, reports and revelations.

Many of these cases were from our area and involved many with whom we'd gone to school or we'd known in other ways.

There was little early accountability by the Church in these investigations. The strategy seemed to be one of cover-up and concealing evidence. This piled on more pain and suffering to those who were abused, many of whom had experienced long-term trauma, including severe emotional distress, depression, anxiety and, in some cases, suicide. Many reported feelings of shame and isolation due to the stigma associated with speaking out against the Church and its subsequent denial. The abuse and lack of accountability severely damaged public trust in the Catholic Church and prompted many to leave it altogether.

In our area of West Donegal, the level of historic abuse reported was very high. In 1997, a local priest reported to Gardai (the Irish police) that he was being blackmailed for money. The aftermath of this incident resulted in that priest being charged and convicted for 26 counts of sexual abuse, with many more suspected. At the same time, a local schoolteacher who was known to us was convicted on more than 50 charges of child abuse. Other cases emerged, mainly due to the outstanding, thorough and compassionate investigation by Garda Sergeant Martin Ridge. His work and that of other Gardai resulted in prosecutions.

The Church was certainly not proactive in its accountability. It only acted, at a very slow pace, when investigations from outside sources made it no longer possible to deny or cover up serious abuse and mistreatment of those unable to defend themselves or others intimidated by the power of the Church. This was a dark period and one that had a deep impact. I wasn't abused myself but, in many ways, I feel that we were all betrayed by rogue priests and the Church. I would include in that betrayal good priests who were let down by an institution that called on them to act with integrity yet, when tested, did not do so themselves.

Musings from Madonna's Caravan

It's said the darkest hour is the one just before dawn. What I've shared above reveals an inconvenient truth about a period that lacked accountability. Over the years there have been considerable strides towards a more accountable society, albeit still imperfect. The introduction of child protection guidelines has created a safer environment, preventing incidents such as those described above from happening on such a large scale again.

Accountability is much more evident in the workplace and the society we live in. There's much more awareness of the importance of holding governments and institutions to account. There's much work to be done in equality, wellbeing, education, housing, responsible consumption, justice and all the areas covered in the United Nations Sustainable Development Goals. However, there's a much greater appetite for accountability and the strong hope that the pains of the past will be somewhat compensated for by a better tomorrow as we ensure that accountability becomes a key element of education, learning and development. The CEO of the credit union who fought to have accountability included in their programme for staff as well as the senior management team at the Mater Hospital who insisted on the same had great foresight and vision, and I thank them for that.

Chapter 6

Diversity

Diversity refers to the presence of differences within a given setting, such as at home or in the workplace, community or society. These differences can be based on various characteristics, including but not limited to:

→ race and ethnicity: different racial and ethnic backgrounds

→ gender: different gender identities and expressions

→ age: people of various age groups and life stages

→ sexual orientation: individuals with different sexual preferences and identities

→ disability: physical or mental impairments and differing abilities

→ socioeconomic background: various social, economic and educational backgrounds

→ culture: different cultural practices, languages and values

→ religion or belief systems: different religious beliefs or spiritual practices

→ neurodiversity: the concept that neurological differences such as those associated with autism, ADHD, dyslexia, dyspraxia and other conditions are natural variations in the human brain rather than disorders that need to be fixed or cured.

Too often, I fall into the feeling that diversity is a modern term or something that I must be more conscious of, but in truth it has always been hugely important. Difference challenges us, but without that challenge, we'd surely remain fixed in the mindset that diversity and the acceptance of it is difficult and therefore we're better off staying in our fixed state of thought. It's easier and more comfortable to associate with someone who feels familiar, whether that's because they're from your community, speak the same language, know people that you know, have the same level of education or have other things in common. Growth, however, doesn't happen in this comfort zone and therefore we're challenged to move out of it and into a changing world of globalisation where technology, war, work and freedom have brought about a much greater movement of people to many different parts of the world. The global movement of people as well as increased connectivity means that embracing diversity has never been as important. The challenges here can be addressed by greater awareness and the inclusion of diversity training in education and workplace learning.

Closer to home

As I've mentioned in previous chapters, I was born in Elizabeth, New Jersey, and lived there until the age of eight, before moving to Donegal in 1970. Apart from 12 years spent in London, it has been my home ever since. Both my parents and their families go back many generations as people from the Rosses and Gweedore, in West Donegal. On returning to Donegal with my brother John, who was then 18, and my sister Sheila, aged 16, the local area was fascinating to me, in the sense that so many people knew each other and indeed many were related in some way. Going to school in West Donegal was a very different experience from my memory of school in New Jersey. There, my siblings and I had attended a Catholic school and at that time, in the 1960s, I was conscious that it was predominantly white, with most children having Irish, Italian and Polish parents or grandparents. My father, who was working towards a qualification as a plumber, was a big boxing fan and adored Cassius Clay, who later changed his name to Muhammad Ali. In many ways this was my first introduction to someone who had a different skin colour. I'd hear my father talk about this 'great young black kid' who would eventually be the greatest boxer of all time. Muhammad Ali was not only different because of the colour of his skin, he also challenged authority, something that wasn't easy in 1960s America. He was also funny and confident. He was extremely talented and dedicated to his sport and stood up for his black community yet was equally comfortable with white people of all classes. His personality was every bit as big, if not bigger, than his boxing ability. It would be many years before I fully appreciated that observing my father embracing and indeed loving someone 'different' was to make a lasting impression on me.

I settled quickly into school and community life in Ireland. This was aided by relations and friends from my small townland, who saw it as their duty to explain the patterns and traditions in their own way. I learned the Irish language (Gaeilge) quickly, mainly because there was a grant of £1,000 available for my parents to build a house, as long as the children in the family could speak the language. A house then cost about £4,000 to build, so getting 25 per cent of that cost in the form of a grant was a big help. Soon after going to primary school, a dispute broke out about the level of the Irish language being spoken in what was then an amalgamated school. Those who didn't speak Irish were simply from areas where it had died out, and those who did speak it did so because it was strong and vibrant in their communities. But the dispute brought about the picketing of our school and subsequent national TV coverage. It was long and drawn out as the main topic of conversation, and as a result it fuelled great division in our community. The Irish language and its use by some and not by others was my first experience of difference and division and the negative impact of diversity when it creates a cultural collision.

Both sport and music were a big part of my youth, as they were for the circle of friends I had in those early and teenage years. Sport was confined to soccer and Gaelic football, which is a more rugged and rougher game. Those who played locally were all from the immediate locality. Again, they were all Irish and in nearly all cases their families had lived in the area for generations. Discos and dances were dominated by a very similar breakdown of mostly girls and boys from the locality along with the children of Irish emigrants who'd moved to Glasgow, whom we affectionately referred to as 'Scotties', and who'd arrive in June to spend the summer months in Donegal. Occasionally, someone born in another country to an Irish parent would arrive at school or into the community. They were considered an exception and as such their arrival was handled with confusion, uncertainty and a mixed reaction. In hindsight, it's easy to see how little diversity there was in West Donegal in the 1970s. Radio Luxembourg, Radio Caroline and *Top of the Pops* brought us alternative music from the explosion of great artists in the UK and US. Just like music, sport was another divergent influence into our teenage brains. The predominantly Catholic education system had tried its best to ensure we didn't lose our religion to outside influences, but our interest in British soccer teams and great players such as George Best, Charlie George, Bobby Charlton and Bobby Moore, as well as music from Madness, Squeeze, the Police and the Drifters, brought more colour and variety into our lives. Religion was going to have to work very hard if it was to discourage us from looking at Sheena Easton or John Travolta as popular icons.

In 1980, a new Gaelic football club was formed in our area. Diversity would bring together parts of the parish that had been split in the Irish language school dispute years earlier. In hindsight, this was a big task, yet it was led by trusted leaders who hadn't been directly involved in the divisive nature of this previous issue. The entire club membership and involvement was male. We'd all have known each other as we'd have played on different teams or against each other in the past. If not, we soon got to know those with whom we'd be playing as the club found its awkward feet in those early years. The Irish language issue was abating for two reasons. One was that those of us who didn't speak the language fluently had our own respect for it and therefore looked with envy as opposed to anger at those who spoke it well. The second reason was that the younger Irish-speaking generation now playing football with us could switch to English with great comfort and would therefore remove the barriers of the past.

Over the years, the Irish language and its survival and indeed growth in our club has been great to witness. Respect has played a big part in that. Alongside it, the diversity of our club, now just over 40 years old, has been dramatic. At least 40 per cent of the club membership is female. The club has girls' teams at all levels from under tens to senior ladies. The club committee, once a bastion of grumpy men in a smoke-filled room in the local pub because there was no clubhouse, is now most likely to be 50 per cent female in a well-appointed clubroom overlooking the state-of-the-art football pitch with floodlights.

The local Irish-only born and bred nature of those involved in bringing the club forward is changing as well. Mothers, fathers, partners and individuals from all parts of the world who have, for different reasons, moved to the area, are involved in different aspects of club activities, which is much more about the development of competent, confident children and not just about winning matches. The diversity here, although often slow to develop, has been progressive and to the absolute benefit of the club and the community. It's a thriving club, voted club of the year in recent years for its facilities, service to the community and overall example of a best practice model of inclusion and belonging.

Musings from Madonna's Caravan

There have always been two memories of school that I was somewhat uncomfortable with. One was when some students were called out of class by a visiting teacher. They were openly referred to as 'slow learners'. Strong and less sympathetic words were used to describe the students in the playground. Another uncomfortable experience happened weekly, and that was during a class on religion. The vast majority of those who attended our school were Catholic. However, the Boyds from nearby Carrickfin were Church of Ireland and hence Protestants. For our religion class, the Boyds were excluded and invited to 'go out to play'. For an hour, they'd go outside, make up games but often look through the windows while it was raining as we enjoyed shelter and warmth while being told about the 'loving God for all'. I thought these occurrences at school were cruel and certainly shaped my opinion of both education and religion.

The religious element in Ireland has since lost its control and reach and whereas those who wish to practise it can do so freely, those who seek their spirituality in different ways aren't seen as outcasts. Where we still have much to do is in the area of neurodiversity. The 'slow learners' that were removed weekly from our class were most likely neurodiverse. I watched as they left school and some were extremely driven and talented. Others created businesses that employed numerous people and had great resilience and the ability to navigate through complex work situations. Some went on to create companies involved in well-known global projects. Some stayed at home, kept the fires and ran the GAA club activities. Sadly, one, an extremely driven person who twice swam around Ireland among other work-related achievements, took his own life as he approached 60. These were misunderstood people and as such excluded from the rest of 'us', who were no more talented or able, but didn't have autism, ADHD, dyslexia, dyspraxia and other conditions we're only now becoming more aware of. Education and indeed society must move much more quickly to ensure that neurodiversity is understood and catered for within a system that has failed it.

The discussion, awareness and teaching of diversity, equality, inclusion and belonging is vital for a better Donegal, Ireland and world. Like many skills needed for the future, diversity is not only a human skill but also a call for a better humanity. In the words of Nobel Peace Prize winner John Hume in 1998, 'Difference is of the essence of humanity. Difference is an accident of birth and it should therefore never be the source of hatred or conflict. The answer to difference is to respect it. Therein lies a most fundamental principle of peace: respect for diversity.'

Chapter 7
Emotional intelligence

Many credit American psychologist and author Daniel Goleman as the modern-day thought leader on the subject and skill of emotional intelligence. Goleman argues that for success, character, happiness and lifelong achievements, emotional intelligence (EQ) is just as, if not more, important than purely cognitive abilities that have always been measured by more conventional IQ tests. His early work from 1995 (published in his classic book *Emotional Intelligence*) has been hugely supported since as a challenge to educators and skills trainers to recognise and include more emotional intelligence learning in modern curricula. However, long before Goleman, Aristotle (who died in 322 BC), made a philosophical observation when he said: 'Anyone can become angry – that is easy. But to be angry with the right person, to the right degree, at the right time, for the right purpose, and in the right way – that is not easy.'

In our CSEI study of human skills for the future of work, emotional intelligence often emerges as a skill that's either requested by participants or mentioned by employers. EQ involves recognising, understanding and managing our own emotions and the emotions of others. According to Goleman's model, the key components of emotional intelligence are as follows:

1. Self-awareness

→ the ability to recognise and understand your own emotions

→ awareness of how your emotions affect your thoughts and behaviours

→ knowing your strengths, weaknesses and triggers.

2. Self-regulation

→ the ability to manage and control your emotions, impulses and reactions

→ staying calm and composed in stressful situations

→ practising self-discipline, thoughtfulness and adaptability.

3. Motivation

→ the drive to pursue goals with energy and persistence

→ a strong desire to achieve and a commitment to personal growth

→ resilience and maintaining a positive attitude, even in the face of setbacks.

4. Empathy

→ the ability to understand and share the feelings of others

→ being aware of others' emotions and responding appropriately

→ effective listening and considering other perspectives.

5. Social skills

→ the ability to build and maintain healthy relationships

→ effective communication, conflict resolution and cooperation

→ influencing others, leadership abilities and working well in teams.

These components work together to help individuals navigate social complexities, make better decisions and achieve personal and professional success. If these EQ skills and attributes are considered to be important in the world of work, we're certainly not near the mark in terms of the education and training of these key skills. Imagine if we could improve the EQ of everyone in the world by 10 per cent? How much would that add to the quality of life both economically and socially?

Closer to home

Understanding emotions certainly wasn't a subject in the primary or secondary schools in the Ireland of the 1970s and 1980s. We certainly had emotions but the best you could do was to try to figure it all out as you went along. My parents, like most from the rugged Rosses region, both emigrated in their teenage years to Scotland to work in potato fields, building sites, tunnels, fish processing, hotel work and anywhere they could find work recommended by others whom they knew. My father lost his mother when he was just two years old, and my mother's father died when she was a year old. As I first mentioned in Chapter 3, when both my parents were in their early teens, a mine exploded in a nearby shoreline townland, killing 19 young boys and men, many of whom had been at school with them earlier that day. The aftermath of the Ballymanus disaster had a devastating effect on the local area and there's little doubt that this would have been traumatic for both my parents and many in the close-knit community. There would, of course, have been no psychological support, so dealing with a major trauma would have meant suppressing many of their emotions and getting on with life. Some would have carried the burden and others wouldn't have been able to do as well, which played out in different ways later in their lives.

My parents were married in Glasgow, and later emigrated to America with two children in 1960. I wasn't aware at the time but later understood my mother to be a highly anxious person. This anxiety would play out in different ways. Even when there was nothing wrong of any significance, there was constant drama or an issue. I was too young to understand this and, of course, you didn't talk about such anxiety outside of your home. With my brother and sister now gone from the house and married, I fell into taking blame for the constant anxiety and phantom issues that emerged. This became a pattern of an imagined issue or the heightened description of a minor issue and my acceptance of blame. This was followed by my subsequent feelings of low self-worth and confidence along with trying to compensate for this at school or in community settings by acting as confident yet not feeling so. I wanted to be liked and became a people pleaser and chameleon, telling you what I thought you wanted to hear. Football was an escape of sorts, but I overcompensated by playing out a role that wasn't really authentic. I wasn't particularly talented but found that if I could be rougher and mouthier, I could gain an advantage over others who were perhaps skilful but scared of confrontation or ruggedness. Playing this role allowed me to be part of a team, yet deep down I wasn't comfortable with it.

I had little EQ back then. I'd go on to marry and have six children, but carried a lot of baggage into a hugely responsible role. I didn't have the necessary tools at 20 years of age and the introduction of alcohol certainly fuelled an already decent fire. Alcoholism doesn't give you a guidebook, so the next nine years were not pleasant for any of the participants on that journey and for that, I'm eternally sorry. I was lucky enough to come ashore from drinking at an early enough age but there was and indeed still is a good bit of work to do on myself and my emotional intelligence. Through a 12-step programme, I was able to see the causes of the conflict that had me seeking a solution through alcohol. I discovered that alcohol wasn't the cause of the problem but instead a symptom of a deeper problem or problems. (I'll talk more about this in Chapter 9.)

Through much work on myself, I'd go on to discover that my mother's behaviour was a symptom of narcissism. Narcissus was a figure in Greek mythology known for his extraordinary beauty and self-obsession. According to the myth, he was a young hunter who was so proud of his appearance that he rejected anyone who loved him.

The story takes a tragic turn when Narcissus, seeing his own reflection in a pool of water, falls in love with it, not realising it's merely an image. Unable to leave the beauty of his reflection, he eventually wastes away or drowns, depending on the version of the myth.

The term narcissism is derived from his name and is used in psychology to describe excessive self-love, vanity and a lack of empathy. This lack of empathy was certainly a feature that my mother had, and the self-love and constant measurement of others was not healthy to witness or experience. It may appear critical and uncaring of me to suggest, but this is what I experienced, as well as others in the family. Staying calm and in control through quite often heavy episodes of attack was a big challenge. I often failed in my attempts to not let it impact my work or home life, and the reality is that it caused damage. Emotional intelligence in terms of being aware of what's at play is important, but it doesn't make you bombproof. My mother was really good at recruiting others to collude in her behaviour. Normally these were people loosely connected and predisposed to aiding and abetting such behaviour. They'd offer a sympathetic ear and play the role of rescuer but seldom if ever challenge her behaviour. These 'rescuers' got their satisfaction or fix in playing that role of pulling her into their boat but not showing her how to remain in the boat. This meant that she could do it all again and they could repeat the role of rescuer. If a rescuer tired of the role and lost their commitment, my mother would dismiss them from their role by cutting them off, while having another set of rescuers standing by.

Was this the result of my mother's childhood trauma?

Emotional intelligence

The chances are that it was. There are many other behaviours I could fill a chapter with, but I had to look at the solution for myself and not focus on the problem or issue with her. Anger and resentment are certainly not good strategies, so I was determined to detach from the behaviour, knowing that the unacceptable behaviour was unlikely to change but that I had the power to control my reaction to it. This process was, and still is, arduous. It involves knowing what my triggers are and why they're there. It involves not reacting when the temptation is to do so, and showing compassion, even in the face of attack. This has been a lifelong journey. I've got it wrong a thousand times, and that's why I'm able to get it right now more often than not.

As I write this chapter, my mother is in a nursing home with advanced dementia, which set in rapidly. I visit and she knows me when I do. Her memories are of her childhood and earlier adult years, so I take her there in our conversations, which can be quite informative and interesting. She's relatively happy in these stories and seldom returns to the more troubled parts of her behaviour. It's a healing part of my journey and one that's important. I must lead with compassion and try to understand that someone hitting out is going through a battle that we don't know enough about. We're all impacted by something in our past and for some it's an easy obstacle to overcome, yet for others it becomes a lifelong conflict. Being self-aware and aware of others is therefore of vital importance, and I'd extend this to say even life saving.

Musings from Madonna's Caravan

Emotional intelligence is gathering pace as a measure of character and personality. It relies on our ability to be better human beings with a greater understanding of our own strengths and weaknesses, as well as that of others. To me, the word intelligent used to signify someone who had a degree or was naturally intelligent from reading a lot. As I pass the age of 60, my level of emotional intelligence is in catch-up mode. I'm comfortable with that. I believe that emotional intelligence is a vital basis for continual growth and contentment. Being at peace with the past and the present is vital. Not looking back in anger is important. Choose to not be a victim and start from any point, clearing the wreckage if required, and then march on, motivated by new targets. I believe that emotional intelligence should be a compulsory module of learning at all levels of education.

Chapter 8

Dealing with ambiguity

It's one of the more underrated human skills and yet the ability to deal with ambiguity has become vital in all areas of life, and particularly in a professional context. To consider its importance, we must first look at the meaning of ambiguity and the effect it has in the workplace. According to the Oxford Dictionary, ambiguity is the quality of being open to more than one interpretation, or of being inexact. In simple terms, ambiguity is uncertainty.

In the workplace, ambiguity can be found in a range of contexts, including:

→ behavioural – when actions, intentions or motives are unclear

→ conceptual – when a concept or idea is not clearly defined or understood

→ linguistic – when a word has different meanings or sentence structure can allow for various interpretations

→ situational – when a job role is vague or ill defined, or circumstances within the workplace are unclear.

It's reasonable to expect that a certain level of ambiguity will always be present in the workplace. Answers are not always immediately available, and yet there are occasions when uncertainty can work positively, as it can lead people to think creatively and consider alternative ideas. Accepting that uncertainty is a natural part of business allows for more flexible thinking.

Problems emerge when individuals are faced with uncertainty along with a lack of relevant information and an absence of leadership and collaborative effort. Dealing with complex ambiguous issues on an ongoing basis in high-stakes environments leads to a negative cognitive impact, resulting in problems with mental processes such as thinking, reasoning, memory and decision making. Eventually, this can lead to individual stress and burnout and a culture that's unable to cultivate contentment or success.

The well-known author and management consultant Patrick Lencioni addresses the idea of ambiguity in his work. 'The enemy of accountability is ambiguity' is a quote from his 2002 book *The Five Dysfunctions of a Team: A Leadership Fable*, in which he suggests ambiguity in roles can lead to confusion and a blame culture when things go wrong. Lencioni stresses the importance of well-defined roles to ensure that everyone knows what they're being held accountable for. When team members understand exactly what's expected of them and what success looks like, they're more likely to take ownership of their tasks and be accountable for their outcomes. He also recommends that organisations empower team members to make decisions within their areas of expertise and responsibility and foster a culture whereby challenges are viewed as opportunities. Leaders who can provide clear direction and make decisions even when all the details are not known can help teams to stay aligned and avoid stagnation. Plans can be adjusted as more information becomes available.

Ambiguity can come in many forms in the workplace but it's here to stay. There are many 'unknown unknowns' outside our current knowledge and awareness. Interconnectedness requires businesses to operate in conditions where not all factors are within their control or predictable. Global competition is increasing as markets transcend borders and, as a result, organisations must become more efficient than ever before. There's less time to languish in the often reactive and chaotic start-up stage of innovation and development. The Silicon Valley mantra 'fail fast and fail better' is where innovation meets realism. To evolve through the growth stage, individuals must be prepared for the workforce with key human skills such as dealing with ambiguity. This will equip them to handle the wide range of variables that exist because of globalisation, such as cultural differences, geopolitical risks and different regulatory environments. The modern business landscape requires leaders to deal with digital disruption, Brexit confusion, post-pandemic challenges and global wars with skills that are fast becoming outdated. The challenge of managing ambiguity in the workplace has also been affected by the increasingly diverse nature of the contemporary workforce.

In Ireland, it's estimated that one in ten adults is neurodivergent, a term covering a range of conditions that include attention deficit disorders, autism, dyspraxia and dyslexia. Research suggests that up to 15 to 20 per cent of the population in the United States is neurodivergent. Some might say that every workplace team is neurodiverse, as no two brains are alike, but companies need to set up the workplace to suit a variety of learning styles and cognitive diversities. These are the organisations that will fare the best. By embracing and effectively managing ambiguity through the identification and acknowledgement of issues, organisations can navigate uncertainty and remain competitive. This will enable them to capitalise on new opportunities while having much happier employees. The aim is not to create a rigid workplace culture free of spontaneity, risk and uncertainty, but to embrace the presence of ambiguity and create policies and structures that support employees when it arises.

Closer to home

Moving from the US to rural West Donegal, I was aware of the importance of fishing to the area. Many of my neighbours were employed, year round, on either the boats or in the processing plants, which created many jobs. The previous night's catch of a certain boat was as much a topic of conversation as a football result or the weather. Many kids of my age from secondary school didn't continue their education past the Junior Cert exams and instead went into the fishing industry. Some went on to study at the marine college, others just went to sea, while many others found themselves in the processing plants, handfilleting mackerel on a decent daily rate of pay. The industry demanded hard work in difficult conditions but paid well in return. That money was circulated locally, resulting in a thriving community.

That thriving community was hugely impacted by the introduction of fishing quotas, which are limits set on the amount of fish that can be caught within a specific period, to ensure sustainability and prevent overfishing. The reduction of these quotas affected fishermen and the fishing communities in several ways.

The loss of employment for fishermen had a knock-on effect on processing, maintenance of boats, suppliers, local shops and pubs, hotels and restaurants. Over the course of 20 years, the community witnessed, yet was powerless over, the decline in what had been a vibrant and economically beneficial fishing industry. Ambiguity was rife. Fishermen who were used to simply fishing and looking after their crews, perhaps overextending themselves financially by purchasing bigger boats in the hope of passing on the business to a son, found themselves in a state of uncertainty, huge loss and stress. Politicians and legislators were equally uncertain of their next steps, which were governed by the balance of representing the local community yet answering to legislation being determined by the European Parliament in Brussels.

I have little doubt that this added to a decline in mental wellbeing and therefore increased depression and stress for many. The social fabric of the area was impacted and thriving towns became skeletons of the past as the industry's subsequent decline had a major impact on the economic viability of our community. The perceived injustice among the fishing community certainly caused a delay in looking at alternatives, either finding different species of fish or diversifying into tourism, offshore wind farming and so on. There were many unknown unknowns playing out and uncertainty was tangible as the fishing community sought clarity, which was seldom delivered by those in a position of power and responsibility. Today, there's still a complex transformation taking place in our area of West Donegal and replicated in fishing communities elsewhere in Ireland. While the fishing industry and the associated economic benefits have suffered a decline, tourism and the technological potential have increased. It's difficult, however, for a third-generation fisherman to view his or her future as anything other than what two generations of their family have done before them.

Slowly, there are glimpses of change and transition. Those displaced by the fishing industry are creating opportunities in hospitality with new eateries. Glamping sites have been developed to cater for the many tourists visiting the Wild Atlantic Way, a route along Ireland's Atlantic coastline. Fishing ports such as Killybegs and Burtonport are gradually yet systematically becoming hubs of alternative economies, creating jobs and income for the local and surrounding areas. Technological innovation and start-up infrastructures can potentially encourage those with the skills and mindset from years at sea to transfer these attributes into new and profitable micro-businesses.

Going forward, education and training providers must innovate and understand the skills required for the future of the new working landscape. They must create short and agile learning opportunities to harness the powerful potential from the human resource that those formerly employed in the fishing sector possess. Likewise, governments must inject investment into communities that feel abandoned. This potential, matched by the resilience of the fishing community, can lead to a powerful rebirth after an ambiguous period.

In 2022, work-based learning expert Dr Oran Doherty and I met with George Westerman, a professor at MIT in Boston and a global voice on the skills of the future. That all sounds very impressive and good for my ego, but in truth it was a simple meeting of minds. Dr Doherty was born in the village next to mine, but we didn't meet until many years later. MIT had recently completed its research on the Human Skills Matrix, comprising 24 human skills deemed vital for the future of work. Among the 24 skills was one that stated simply 'comfort with ambiguity'. Over coffee, tea and, later, pizza, Westerman explained the importance of learning to deal with ambiguity as a key human skill. The more examples he gave of large corporations such as Microsoft, the more I thought of the fishing community back in Donegal. I believe God works in mysterious ways and the universe often opens channels to something else. Two weeks after the Boston trip, having just learned about the concept of dealing with ambiguity, my small but energetic business won a contract to investigate the feasibility of creating a Blueway between Burtonport and Arranmore Island, both areas impacted heavily and negatively by fishing quotas. A Blueway is a successful and high-quality trail of activities based in or around water, proven to create revenue and employment while promoting sustainable connections with nature. This concept has the potential to create up to 150 jobs while increasing the wellbeing of the local and visiting population. Since the feasibility study was carried out, Blueway status has been achieved and, in the future, we'll see the development of a magnificent Blueway region, the first of its kind in Europe. Not only does it have the potential to correct the job losses that arose from the decline of fishing but, more importantly, it will also enhance people's wellbeing.

As a result, the human skill of dealing with ambiguity is one that I have faith in. I believe that, through a Human Skills Institute, our workshops can assist organisations anywhere in the world to navigate change and uncertainty with short and relevant courses that include the following ideas:

→ **Embrace ambiguity** as an opportunity for growth and learning. Adopting a mindset that values curiosity and adaptability can help you approach uncertain situations with openness and resilience.

→ While ambiguity may be unavoidable at times, **actively seek clarity** by asking questions, gathering information from good sources and clarifying expectations or objectives. Communication plays a crucial role in reducing ambiguity.

→ **Targeted attention:** identify specific areas of uncertainty and focus on addressing them systematically.

→ **Explore different perspectives:** engage in and allow for diverse viewpoints and consider alternative interpretations.

→ **Stay flexible** and be prepared to adjust your approach as new information or circumstances emerge. Flexibility is key to navigating ambiguity and responding to unexpected changes.

→ **Develop the skills of problem solving** by practising critical thinking and evaluating potential outcomes. Having a structured approach to problem solving can enhance confidence in dealing with ambiguity.

→ **Manage stress and uncertainty:** build resilience and coping mechanisms to manage the stress associated with ambiguity. Mindfulness, self-care activities and supporting one another in the workplace are all important.

→ **Embrace experimentation:** taking risks can often uncover solutions and reduce ambiguity. Embrace and encourage a culture of experimentation. There's no innovation without failure. Learn from trial and error.

→ **Control the controllables:** not all aspects of ambiguity are within your control. Instead of fixating on uncertainties, concentrate on actions and decisions that you can influence or manage.

In summary, learning to act without knowing all the details is a key component in dealing with ambiguity.

Musings from Madonna's Caravan

The uncertainty in the fishing industry in West Donegal over the past 30 years has been an example of ambiguity seen through the lens of my own life. It's a profession that always seemed unclear and ill defined. Fishermen had to handle the stress of not knowing what was ahead in terms of the quotas of fish they were allowed to catch, and the fishing of species such as salmon was stopped completely.

Although the ins and outs of environmental considerations and imbalanced quota distribution can be debated, one thing that's clear is that the decline of the fishing industry deeply impacted our community in many ways. Those involved lost not only their livelihoods and sense of purpose but also their identity. For many there was no plan B, simply because of a complete lack of clarity around the eventual outcome. The story of the decline is one in which the leadership within the sector and from policymakers and politicians was severely lacking.

However, communities can be resilient, especially the fishing community, which is no stranger to adversity, and at present the community response in West Donegal has been strong. Tourism is increasing and, as a result, the area is transforming and adapting to its potential while not impacting negatively on the environment. Technology offers another source of hope and we're already seeing sprouting seeds emerge where businesses based in West Donegal can trade globally, creating jobs and inspiration. Innovation hubs are being supported by European Union funds.

For me personally, it has been interesting to bear witness to these changes as a business start-up. Acting without a script or all the details is commonplace and yet dealing with ambiguity remains a challenge for many. But it's a challenge that must be faced to protect the sustainability of rural areas such as my own. The answer to the problem is to create an environment where alternatives are available. That requires a new awareness and an education that transfers the skills and knowledge across from fishing to new and emerging sectors such as tourism and technology.

It also requires that those displaced fishermen are part of the solution, so that their legacy is a positive one. Funding to support these changes is vital, so the politicians and those in a position to impact change are accountable for their responsibilities. Amid this ambiguity lie the seeds of opportunity.

Chapter 9

Conflict management

Conflict management is a key component of management in the workplace. But dealing effectively with conflict in our personal lives can also make for better, stronger and more satisfying relationships. Such is the nature of life that disagreements are an inevitable, normal and healthy part of relating to people. How we handle them is the part we need to get right.

I've long believed that conflict management should be an essential module taught in school at secondary and third level. For example, a student studying civil engineering will attend university for four years, learning the technical aspects of engineering through the heavily directed STEM subjects (science, technology, engineering, maths), which prepares them, theoretically at least, for employment. However, without any conflict management knowledge and skills, the student won't be prepared for the conflicting and often chaotic environment of the construction site or large road project they find themselves involved in. This is a huge gap in their education, and it can have an adverse effect on the student as they work to fit into the workplace.

This example is also relevant to other sectors as well as social and domestic situations.

Conflict varies from international territorial issues that lead to war to a difference in values between two people that cause tension at work or home. It can arise from strongly held moral or ethical beliefs or a lack of resources where essentials such as water, food or money are scarce. Power dynamics occur in cases where one group holds more power over another and often where the less powerful group feels marginalised and excluded. Fear, brought on by feelings of threat, whether real or perceived, can lead to defensive or aggressive behaviours that result in conflict.

From my own experience, fear is the greatest cause of conflict and is centred around a fear of not getting what you want or losing something you have. When fear is present among groups of people, conflict can become uncontrollable and difficult to contain. It's also the cause of many other forms of internal conflict, which presents as addiction such as alcoholism. When addiction is a feature in the home, socially or in the workplace, it's not always obvious, and the addict can be cunning, baffling and powerful in their negative behaviour. We must also acknowledge that there are those who are addicted to drama and the part they play in it.

While the causes of conflict are wide ranging, the awareness and management of conflict has become an important area of research and study. It's becoming increasingly pertinent that, as the workplace becomes more digitally driven, the over-reliance on technology is moving us away from human, social interaction and hence the ability to have difficult conversations is becoming diminished. To test the need for conflict management learning, CSEI conducted a cross-sector survey in 2024, asking if conflict management should form part of the curriculum for third-level degree courses and lifelong and work-based learning programmes. Figures showed that 97 per cent supported the idea, with 15 per cent suggesting that it depended on the sector.

In looking into the solutions and the best practice conflict management tools available, I've always found the Thomas–Kilmann model to be of value. It suggests that there are simply two approaches to conflict behaviour and that an individual can choose to be either assertive or cooperative in their approach. The model then offers an informative series of options within both approaches, which consist of avoiding, accommodating, competing, compromising and collaborating. Matching the right approach to a particular situation is a skill that takes practice, failure, tweaking and more practice. It would appear from all the evidence as well as the available solutions that conflict management as a human skill is a requirement in life.

Closer to home

On the night of Easter Sunday, 3 April 1983, I had my first alcoholic drink – a vodka and white lemonade – at the Holyrood Hotel in Bundoran, County Donegal. I was 20 years old and getting married the following day. It was a kind of expectation that taking a drink would be part of the night out with those of us heading to Knock Shrine in Mayo, where the wedding was to take place. While I didn't particularly like the taste of the drink, the effect on me was different and positive, or so I thought. I was more relaxed; I believed I was funnier. I sang, joked and had a feeling that took me away from other concerns and issues. My drinking would soon cause problems in the marriage. Before we got married, my wife had never seen me take a drink and never experienced the behaviour that soon accompanied it. For the majority of those who drink alcohol, it represents relaxing with friends and conviviality. But this is not the case with a problem drinker. I wanted to stop drinking on many occasions but failed in my attempts. I became untrustworthy, aggressive, withdrawn, and moved further away from the person I aspired to be. This caused more frustration and the cycle of self-loathing and drinking became embedded.

My problems weren't confined to interpersonal relationships; I was in trouble with the law and had debt problems, too. I blamed outside factors but never the alcohol. Since alcohol was my crutch, there was never a chance that I was going to accept that it was part of the conflict and therefore resisted many calls by family and friends to stop. Was alcohol the cause of the conflict or a symptom of something deeper? The problem drinker or indeed anyone with an addiction becomes cunning, leaving others around them confused and bewildered and often accepting blame, which is part of the manipulation that's a common thread among addicts. I deliberately caused conflict to get the alcohol I craved. Whether I was at work, at home or in the community, I caused disagreements, which made life very difficult for those working and living with me. I recruited others to subtly join in the conflict, which was selfish and damaging to all those who became embroiled in the chaos.

Conflict management

On 12 June 1992, at the age of 29, nine years after that first drink, I was to have my last. I understand that I'm one of the lucky ones, as many problem drinkers continue to consume alcohol for many years and descend into even more hell. I was sick and tired of being sick and tired and fed up with disappointing and hurting those closest to me. I also required help and support as stopping the drinking wasn't the hard bit. Choosing to refrain from drinking every day and dealing with the cause of the obsession and craving was where the work had to be done. That work continues many years later and it centres mainly on dealing with the parts of my character that I want to improve. I try much harder to avoid conflict and pick the battles worth fighting, but I won't avoid conflict if I believe enough in something that I value. As always, balance is the key.

My life as a non-drinker began again at 29 and work, home and social life became easier, but not perfect by any means. At first, I just put down the drink but carried on with the selfishness, which meant that very little changed. It wasn't until after my marriage ended that I realised I needed to look inwards and not to others for the cause of my ongoing issues. Conflict, whether it's inner or concerns others, is like that. Until we look at our part in the problem, resolution is highly unlikely. I needed to clean my own side of the street. All of this represented a profound change.

When I was ten years into sobriety and working and living in London as a manager with a large pub company, an interesting conflict arrived at my door which shaped my thinking. I'd worked with the pub group as an opening manager of new pubs and loved and enjoyed the buzz of it all. At one stage, I was managing three pubs with a great team of 60 staff. We were constantly increasing sales, and this involved a lot of personal development for me and those who were in management positions in other busy south London pubs. After having two good area managers during a five-year period, a new area manager joined the company and within minutes of meeting him, I knew I was in trouble. Many of my subconscious biases were at work, and I disliked the way in which he shook my hand, his poor eye contact and his overall demeanour. In the weeks and months that followed, I didn't connect with this new manager (I'll explain more in Chapter 12). I distanced myself from him, seldom calling him beyond the obligatory Monday morning sharing of weekly figures. He didn't reach out to me either, so the relationship was poor. Neither of us addressed this nor did we acknowledge that there was a problem, choosing instead to avoid a difficult conversation. Then, during one weekly conversation, he made a comment that didn't sit well with me. I asked him to repeat it and he refused, so a series of petty issues subsequently began to evolve into a pattern of constant conflict. I felt I needed to address the issue but didn't feel he was a person I could address it with.

The managing director of the pub group was a civil and decent man, so I went to him informally to explain that I found the new area manager difficult to work with. I did concede that I'd failed to address it sooner, but I felt from the conversation that he'd rather avoid the issue and hoped we could sort it out ourselves. Alongside this it became clear that the culture of the company was changing. There was a focus on squeezing profits out of existing sales and less commitment to sales growth. I was good at the latter but my performance in the former wasn't as confident. I began looking at other work options and found it difficult to give the role I'd enjoyed for five years anything more than minimum effort. This was the most difficult and testing time of my 40-year working life.

I eventually found work elsewhere and left the area manager to what I considered to be his poor management skills and petty behaviour. Up until that point in my career, I'd worked with some inspirational people. But during the six months and the events leading up to leaving my role as area manager, I learned a lot about poor standards and their negative impacts. The biggest lessons for me were about trusting my intuition and not shying away from a difficult conversation, as avoidance isn't always the best solution.

After a year in a new job that was enjoyable but not always fulfilling, I returned to pub management with a newly established pub group. I used the lessons I'd learned from my previous experience to build a better relationship with colleagues. My new area manager and I were both receptive to collaboration and dealt with conflicts jointly using clear and open dialogue and understanding. This benefited our working relationship and ultimately the overall success of the company, and served as a template in conflict management going forward.

Musings from Madonna's Caravan

I've lived in an Ireland full of contradictions. It's a country that has endured much conflict as well as great if imperfect peace. I've also lived in a marriage that was chaotic and troublesome, often of my own making, and I've lived in a marriage of contentment and appreciation of the simple things. I drank alcohol in the presence of many and yet felt empty, lonely and alone, pretending that I was happy. I've been alone and sober with my thoughts, swimming in the Atlantic Ocean in the depths of winter yet savouring every moment. These experiences have shaped my understanding of peace and conflict. I believe that conflict awareness and management are key skills, as we can all benefit from improving our ability to identify problems and find the best approach to dealing with them. This skill is not for managers alone but for each of us. I have a better handle on this than I did 30 years ago, but it's a skill that requires lifelong learning and one that I hope to improve on even further.

Chapter 10

Teamwork

There are fewer things more interesting to me than watching teams perform well. As I've said before, success leaves clues, and there are certain attributes that successful teams have that are missing from teams that don't enjoy the same success. I'm a sports enthusiast and believe that in business we owe a lot to sport, especially team sports. There are so many examples of greatness, be that in rugby with the success of the All Blacks from 2000 to 2010, American football's New England Patriots from 2001 to 2019, in football with Brazil between 1958 and 1970 (a period known as the Pele era), or Barcelona FC during 2008–2012 under the management of Pep Guardiola.

Even though Muhammad Ali, Michael Phelps, Serena Williams, Tiger Woods, Rafael Nadal, Jackie Joyner-Kersee and Usain Bolt may be seen as individual sporting successes, all had teams around them supporting and driving their achievements. In business, companies such as Google, Microsoft, Apple, Zappos, Toyota, Netflix and Pixar are known to focus greatly on teamwork. I've also seen its relevance through my own experiences. In 1998, while working in London, I attended a two-day Belbin Team Roles course. Developed by Dr Meredith Belbin, the concept identifies nine distinct roles that people tend to adopt when working in teams. These roles are categorised into three main groups: action oriented, people oriented and thought oriented. Each role has strengths and allowable weaknesses that contribute to team dynamics and success. Here's a summary of the nine roles:

Action-oriented roles:

Shaper

- *Strengths:* Dynamic, challenging, thrives under pressure, drives the team forward.
- *Weaknesses:* Can be prone to provocation, may sometimes be argumentative.

Implementer

- *Strengths:* Practical, efficient, disciplined, turns ideas into action.
- *Weaknesses:* Can be inflexible, resists change.

Completer finisher

- *Strengths:* Detail-oriented, conscientious, ensures thorough completion of tasks, perfectionist.
- *Weaknesses:* May worry too much, tends to focus on minor details.

People-oriented roles:

Coordinator

→ *Strengths:* Confident, clarifies goals, promotes decision making, delegates effectively.

→ *Weaknesses:* Can be seen as manipulative, tends to delegate too much work.

Team worker

→ *Strengths:* Cooperative, diplomatic, supportive, builds relationships, helps the team gel.

→ *Weaknesses:* Indecisive in crunch situations, avoids confrontation.

Resource investigator

→ *Strengths:* Enthusiastic, outgoing, explores external opportunities, develops contacts.

→ *Weaknesses:* Overoptimistic, can lose interest once initial enthusiasm fades.

Thought-oriented roles:

Plant

→ *Strengths:* Creative, innovative, solves difficult problems, generates new ideas.

→ *Weaknesses:* Can be impractical, tends to ignore details, can be too preoccupied to communicate effectively.

Monitor evaluator

→ *Strengths:* Logical, impartial, makes judgements, weighs pros and cons.

→ *Weaknesses:* Lacks enthusiasm, can be overly critical.

Specialist

→ *Strengths:* Dedicated, provides in-depth knowledge and expertise in a specific area.

→ *Weaknesses:* Limited to a narrow field, may focus too much on technical details.

Key points:

→ A successful team often includes a mix of these roles, ensuring that the team benefits from diverse strengths and compensates for individual weaknesses.

→ Individuals can perform more than one role but usually have one or two natural preferences.

This course had a big impact on my life in several ways. One was a hunger to study more of the Belbin Team Roles concept, as it made a lot of sense in a very practical way. Successful teams require difference, not sameness. Years later, I read a book that was highly recommended to me called *The Barcelona Way* by Damian Hughes (2018, now withdrawn), which explores the success of FC Barcelona by examining the cultural and leadership principles behind the club's achievements during its golden era, particularly under coach Pep Guardiola. The book delves into the concept of 'cultural architects', influential individuals who shape an organisation's success through shared values, leadership and a unified vision. Hughes discusses how the values at FC Barcelona, such as humility, effort, ambition, respect and teamwork, played a key role in building a winning culture. He also highlights how these principles can be applied to other organisations, not just in sports but also in business and leadership contexts.

The principles in *The Barcelona Way* are not new but they were highlighted in the glory years enjoyed by the club, following many unsuccessful years. Damian Hughes made an extremely strong case in his book that a compelling vision matched by a strong culture were the basic requisites for their success. Barcelona's broader vision, '*Més que un club*' (more than a club), represented a commitment not only to footballing success but to embodying values of humility, unity and sportsmanship. Guardiola's team was the embodiment of this ethos. They played beautiful football, but the vision was as much about teamwork, respect and selflessness as it was about winning trophies. Exceptional footballers who played at the club at that time had to understand the vision and values and were expected to protect the culture through their behaviours both on and off the pitch.

The principles of creating a strong and compelling vision and having values that inform the behaviour of an organisation provide the basis for good teamwork and impact. Sport can also get inspiration from great business successes, as long as that success is measurable. We're witnessing a shift from all-out profit and shareholder benefit to sustainable business models where people, profit and the planet are all part of what success is deemed to be.

Closer to home

The morning of 10 April 1998 was a tense, emotional and historic moment in Ireland's history. At that time I was living in Canterbury, Kent, and like practically everyone with an Irish connection and indeed many without, I was glued to the overnight news reports from Belfast. I'd taken the evening and following day off work as I wanted to witness the possibility of history being made. The negotiations, which had taken place at Stormont in Belfast, were the culmination of years of peace talks aimed at ending decades of sectarian conflict known as the Troubles. The morning unfolded as follows.

By the morning of 10 April, the talks had extended beyond their original deadline of the previous night. Negotiations had gone on through the night, and there was immense pressure to reach a deal. Political leaders from both Northern Ireland and the UK, along with an exceptional human being, US Senator George Mitchell, who played a key role as mediator, were heavily involved in the discussions. The inability of news teams to give updates due to information blackouts added to a fear that this might all fall through.

Many of the political leaders, including British Prime Minister Tony Blair, Irish Taoiseach Bertie Ahern and Northern Ireland party leaders were exhausted after days of intense, emotionally charged talks. The atmosphere was filled with anxiety and uncertainty about whether a final agreement would be reached. Unionists, Loyalists, Republicans, Nationalists, many not talking to each other, were tired and jaded yet in many ways felt, as Tony Blair described in an intuitive quote, 'I feel the hand of history upon our shoulder with respect to this, I really do.'

As the morning progressed, I sat in my small flat and watched the live coverage on the BBC, as I had through the night, with a few short bouts of sleep in between. Soon, a breakthrough was achieved. The agreement was carefully worded to balance the various political factions. It included provisions for the future governance of Northern Ireland, power-sharing arrangements, decommissioning of weapons and the release of political prisoners. The deal was brokered after key compromises were made on sensitive issues such as the status of Northern Ireland and the nature of policing and justice.

As the sun rose on that Good Friday morning in Belfast, the leaders knew they were on the brink of a momentous occasion. Once finalised, the Good Friday Agreement (also known as the Belfast Agreement) marked a new chapter in Northern Ireland's history, laying the groundwork for peace after 30 years of violent conflict. The agreement was signed later that day, ushering in a period of relative peace and cooperation in Northern Ireland.

I vividly remember sitting in the flat on my own but standing up when the news broke through of an agreement being reached. This was a different feeling to the football victories for Ireland or Donegal. This was a rawer emotion, deep and proud that Irish people of all religions and none, those who despised and killed, those who sought peaceful means and those who committed to the process to ensure a better tomorrow for all sides, had just brought our complex and complicated island hope, moving us away from more than 30 years of killing. The uniqueness of that feeling will never leave me. I started ringing people I knew would be equally invested in the previous 12 hours and would also have stayed up. Some were every bit as excited as I was and one or two had fallen asleep during the night and my call had awakened them with the news. That was the only anticlimax of that day.

This was the greatest example of teamwork I'd ever seen. Every success is an imperfect one. The Good Friday Agreement wasn't without its difficulties. Ian Paisley's Democratic Unionist Party (DUP) boycotted the talks. There were breakdowns in negotiations at crucial times, moments of tension and ongoing challenges with implementing parts of the agreement. Not everyone would share in the joy; there would be those who felt left out. However, the collective effort to overcome these obstacles illustrates how teamwork can achieve results even in the most challenging of circumstances.

The Good Friday Agreement is seen historically and globally as a best practice example of outstanding teamwork, especially in the context of conflict resolution and political negotiation. The teamwork involved in reaching the agreement was complex and multi-faceted, requiring cooperation across various deeply divided groups, both within Northern Ireland and internationally.

Key elements of teamwork that contributed to the success of the Good Friday Agreement are as follows:

→ **Cross-community collaboration:** the agreement brought together opposing sides in Northern Ireland, particularly the Unionists (who were largely Protestant and wanted Northern Ireland to remain part of the UK) and Nationalists (mostly Catholic, seeking a united Ireland). These groups had been in conflict for decades during the Troubles, making the teamwork required for agreement ground-breaking.

→ **Involvement of multiple stakeholders:** it involved not just political leaders from Northern Ireland (such as the Ulster Unionist Party, Sinn Féin and the Social Democratic and Labour Party) but also the British and Irish governments. The teamwork across national boundaries was crucial in facilitating a compromise.

→ **International mediation:** the United States played an important specialist mediating role, with figures such as US Senator George Mitchell acting as chair of the talks. The teamwork across nations demonstrated how external facilitators can help broker peace in deeply divided regions.

→ **Negotiation and compromise:** the agreement is often viewed as a triumph of negotiation and compromise. Teams from various political factions had to set aside deeply held differences to agree on power-sharing arrangements, the decommissioning of paramilitary weapons and the creation of new governmental institutions.

→ **Vision of a shared goal:** the overarching vision was peace and a stable future for Northern Ireland. While the teams involved had very different visions for what that future would look like, they were able to align with the need to end violence and create a political framework for peace. When the talks struggled, the chair would bring them back to the compelling vision of a stable Northern Ireland.

→ **Values:** trust, honesty, transparency, respect and dialogue were crucial elements of the efforts involved.

The Good Friday Agreement demonstrated teamwork and diversity in action.

Musings from Madonna's Caravan

Teamwork is essential in any organisation as it fosters collaboration, leverages diverse strengths and drives efficiency and innovation. In a team environment, individuals can share different perspectives, which leads to more creative problem solving and better decision making. Here are the key reasons why teamwork is important:

→ **Shared responsibility:** teamwork spreads the workload, reducing pressure on any single person and allowing the team to achieve more together.

→ **Better problem solving:** combining different skills, experiences and viewpoints leads to more comprehensive solutions to complex problems.

→ **Enhanced communication:** working as a team improves communication skills, ensuring that everyone is aligned and understands their role in achieving common goals.

→ **Increased motivation and support:** team members often motivate and support each other, fostering a positive environment where individuals are encouraged to perform at their best.

For those who aren't natural team players and may be more comfortable working alone, the support of the team is critical. They can benefit from:

→ **learning from others** – adopting teamwork skills such as collaboration and compromise by observing colleagues

→ **building trust** – teamwork helps to build trust over time, creating an environment where individuals feel valued and respected, which often softens resistance to teamwork

→ **skills development** – non-team players may be skilled individually, but teamwork can help them develop new skills such as communication, adaptability and conflict resolution.

It's important not to view outstanding teamwork only in places such as the Nou Camp Stadium, home of FC Barcelona, or inside the Stormont building where the Good Friday Agreement took place. Teamwork is important in every community group, small and medium business, cafe, shop, public service office and indeed anywhere where people are working or playing together. At a time when we're faced with an increased need to look after those around us, teamwork can play a significant role in supporting positive mental health. Being part of a team provides a sense of belonging and reduces feelings of isolation. Human connection is an antidote to stress, anxiety and depression. Working in a team encourages open communication and problem solving, which can help individuals express their feelings, seek help when needed and develop emotional intelligence.

By focusing on, investing in and promoting teamwork into various aspects of life, whether in professional settings or social contexts, we can greatly support an individual's mental wellbeing. Imagine a world where we can learn to support each other professionally and socially and use our strengths within a team while others can help us with our 'allowable weaknesses', as Belbin frames them. These investments in teamwork can lead to increased productivity, innovation and economic growth, as well as improved social outcomes such as reduced inequality, improved health and wellbeing and greater social cohesion. Once again, this would be putting people first. These are prizes too big to ignore. Let's do better, not for winning alone but for humanity itself.

Chapter 11

Growth mindset

A growth mindset is the belief that your ability and intelligence can be developed through effort, learning and perseverance. It builds on the adage of 'mind over matter' but is much more than that. People with a growth mindset see challenges as opportunities to grow rather than reasons to stop. They view failure as part of the learning process and believe they can improve through hard work, effective strategies and help from others. Embedded as a value in an organisation or business, a growth mindset can have a profound impact on objectives and results.

In my examination of this human skill, first popularised by American psychologist Carol S Dweck (2012), there are several key elements that can be used as a framework for best practice:

→ **Embrace challenges:** view obstacles as opportunities to learn and grow.

→ **Learn from criticism:** see feedback as useful and informative rather than a personal attack.

→ **Persist through difficulties:** don't give up easily

→ **Effort as a path to success:** understand that effort is necessary to achieve higher levels of ability.

→ **Celebrate others' success:** rather than feeling threatened, find inspiration and learn from others.

For most people, a growth mindset is not the default. Perhaps it's not even reasonable to suggest such a mindset can be sustained on a constant basis. Mistakes and failure are an inevitable part of life, but it's how you approach and learn from them that matters. By developing a growth mindset, you can train the mind to see challenges as opportunities and reward the journey, not the destination.

Closer to home

I certainly didn't always embrace a growth mindset. During my period of heavy drinking between the ages of 20 and 30, my choices were aligned with criticism and gossip. I was swimming in a messy bog of negativity and was happy to surround myself with others who tried hard to keep afloat by pulling others down.

However, this elevated sense was temporary and shallow. I couldn't see that at the time, but it became a 'poor me' collective whose members thought the world was working against them. Even calling it a fixed mindset seems too complimentary. A siege mentality is a more accurate representation. I wasn't conscious that I was bringing this negative mindset into work, home and the community groups I was involved with. Occasionally and with some energy, I could rise above it and show flashes of positivity or aspects of a growth mindset, but I'd inevitably return to the fixed and indeed toxic place, particularly if I was struggling with the project or task at hand. I would then criticise the success of it because I wasn't centrally involved. I was threatened by the success of others even though, deep within, I could see the benefits they were creating. It was a conflicting place to be. In hindsight, it was a dark and damaging place inside my head. Growth mindset versus fixed mindset wasn't a topic of conversation or education at that time. In any case, I wasn't ready to measure myself against it as it would have shone a light on the darkness, which at that time was a place of comfort for me. Although, on reflection, it was far from comfortable.

Anyone recovering from an addiction will know that it's the cause of the conflict that must be addressed and not simply the substance (drink, drugs, gambling, etc). There are many who possess a fixed mindset and addiction isn't obvious. The need for drama is also an addiction of sorts and there are people who create drama to feed their own need for it. Some people reading this chapter may work with or even live with someone who has a fixed mindset, or they may self-identify with a dominant fixed mindset. Self-awareness and the awareness of those around us are important. For me, giving up alcohol wasn't the end of my negative mindset, but it was the catalyst for change. I had to have a long and thorough look at myself through a programme of change that was freely given. I didn't always comply with it or accept it with grace but in time I felt and could see the impact of the change. I was no longer satisfied with being unhappy. At my core I'm a positive person but I was playing out a negative or fixed mindset in all aspects of my life. Throw alcohol on top of that and it's the nearest to hell on Earth I can describe.

I've been on community or club committees where there have been those who resist growth or progress simply because change scares them. There are many reasons for this, which would require a book of their own to outline. However, a constant, fixed mindset based on negative thoughts and actions limits growth and progress. Too often it's not called out, simply because those who wish to see progress, change and improvement don't receive the required support from those who sit passively and fail to challenge those with a fixed mindset. For me, change was slow but steady. I left behind the negatives as best as I could.

In 1998, I was a manager with the O'Neill's pub group in London. The pub was undergoing a major refurbishment and we were able to put the time and a decent budget to good use to train all 25 or so staff. I'm unsure about how the idea emerged, but I decided the theme of the training would be to create and deliver a service standard that would be world class for an Irish pub abroad. At first, the staff were uncertain about this world-class mindset but eventually we used it in all our standard practices. In many ways it became a routine way of working and the accepted standard. We may not always have achieved it, but it was the aspiration or goal that drove our efforts. The outcome was positive – sales were well above projections, profit was above budget, gross margin was up on other pubs in the group and we had a positive working environment, a safe place to work and develop for either part-time or full-time staff.

In 2018, I was appointed by Mayo Sligo and Leitrim Educational Training Board (MSLETB) as a subject matter expert in the creation of a national professional sales apprenticeship. My role was to liaise with industry to see where their professional sales needs were in terms of talent supply. I was also responsible for finding out which skills the industry required from emerging sales talent. As part of a wide steering group that consisted of industry representatives, MSLETB, Quality Qualifications Ireland (QQI) and others, I set the target of creating a world-class professional sales apprenticeship, led by industry and delivered with excellence as a global first. This was an important element of the apprenticeship. By setting a high challenge and ambitious apprenticeship programme, we were able to attract government funding support, industry buy-in and accreditation from the QQI. All stakeholders possessed a growth mindset and ambitious standards in the creation of the curriculum. Now in its seventh year, the national sales apprenticeship continues to be a success story, with young and mature sales professionals going through its two-year work-based learning programme.

More recently, I delivered a leadership programme to the fuel forecourt retailer Applegreen at its new training facility in Portlaoise. The one-day workshop was for managers and assistant managers around the theme of leading customer experience. Applegreen has 14,000 staff in Ireland, the UK and the US, where it's seeing steady growth. As a company, Applegreen has a particular growth mindset. It invests in its people and recruits and retains them well. Going into the workshop, I was conscious of how important the development day was for the managers and ultimately their team members across the sites they represented. My programme was designed with this in mind, and I focused on where the training outcomes could best support their objectives. Plenty of growth mindset activities were included in the training and the response was positive. Along with my support colleague, we were able to identify a young female supervisor who'd entered retail straight from second-level education and wanted to pursue a degree in retail, which we made her aware of. She was energised by the possibility of further development and we were able to praise and recognise her talent in the class by the level of her engagement on the day.

It's important to note that Morgan, the woman in question, had experienced measurement within an education system that relies heavily on progression to the third level, when that route doesn't always support the needs and skill set of a particular individual. Morgan outlined that she was happy in retail and now that a development pathway was possible with the option to study for a degree while continuing in employment, she'd be likely to follow through with her ambition of attaining a senior position within the retail sector. Morgan's story is an example of a growth mindset at work at an individual and personal level and at educator and employment levels, too. It's often a collaborative approach, and when it's widely considered and encouraged, it creates a strong and positive momentum and progress for all.

Musings from Madonna's Caravan

A growth mindset requires effort and practice. I don't believe that my natural default setting is positivity. I can relapse into negativity but my awareness of it has improved greatly. I'm also more tuned into negativity and have little tolerance for it, so can easily back out of it. If on occasion I elect to be negative, I suffer. There have been times when I've failed to overcome those with a fixed mindset and after efforts to do so, have had to move away from the situation, defeated but prepared to learn the lessons.

Adopting a growth mindset and searching for a solution as opposed to dwelling on the problem is a much better place to be. The journey to the solution will have obstacles but having a team and support around you is a big part of overcoming those hurdles. When I'm alone with a problem, I'm not in good company. The need to build trust with others is vital. The need to use those whom you trust is equally so. Sharing the credit for the achievement is important as well as passing it back to others who are on their own journey. A growth mindset is a skill that requires practice and development, but its benefits are wide ranging.

Chapter 12

Effective communication

Of all the human skills, effective communication might be considered the flagship, the keystone. It's the exchange of information that helps us better understand other people and situations; it fosters trust and respect and creates the conditions for sharing creative ideas and solving problems.

A large part of my work in customer experience and leadership training centres on communication. A simple yet effective method I use at the beginning of each seminar invites participants to consider the importance, using percentages, of each of the following three different types of communication:

→ **verbal**: the words we use
→ **vocal**: tone, pace, clarity, energy
→ **non-verbal**: body language.

This concept was developed by psychology professor Albert Mehrabian at the University of California, who explained in his book *Silent Messages* (1971) that non-verbal communication in some circumstances can have more impact than verbal communication.

Setting aside those who have argued against Mehrabian's theory (for example, Morgan 2016), the idea that how we say something has a much greater impact than what we say tends to surprise most people. I've found that there's a lot to be gained from spending time exploring this simple topic through discussion and encouraging participants to play it out through experiential learning. Subsequently, participants often mention in-person communication training as a key learning outcome of the seminar.

How I've communicated in my professional and personal life has been a make-or-break factor in securing and leaving jobs, maintaining healthy relationships and expressing myself in a healthy way. I realise that I'm on a journey of learning and unlearning that includes gaining new skills that help me to continue to improve the way in which I communicate, together with working my way through new technologies that can assist but also negatively impact communication.

The style of successful communicators has changed greatly from what we witnessed in the 19th and 20th centuries. Many of the lauded and inspirational communicators I've looked up to, such as Winston Churchill, John F Kennedy, Martin Luther King, Nelson Mandela, Abraham Lincoln, Barack Obama and Mahatma Gandhi, earned their reputation mainly as leaders through times of crisis and change. But there are modern-day communicators who are redefining leadership in different ways, such as:

Effective communication

→ Brené Brown: empathy and inclusivity
→ Simon Sinek: purpose-driven leadership
→ Malala Yousafzai: transparency and vulnerability.

What unites effective communicators throughout history is their ability to communicate a strong vision and use storytelling to do so. My experience of working with companies across different sectors has proved that the successful communicators of today need to use a variety of human skills. Empathy, accountability and connecting through storytelling are all valuable skills used in effective communication. There's also a case to make that empowerment, growth mindset, decision making and several other human skills included in this book also enhance communication.

As in other aspects of life, when we fail to engage in business, our message is lost. In an age of hyper consumerism, brands must be effective communicators or risk being misunderstood and left behind. Clarity of purpose is becoming as important as product quality and where both combine, we witness success in all its measurements. Effective communication is multi-faceted, requiring a balance of clarity, emotional intelligence, adaptability and gaining feedback. When done well, it builds trust, fosters understanding and leads to successful outcomes in both personal and professional interactions.

Brands that communicate effectively and explain themselves well include:

→ Apple – simplicity, innovation, lifestyle
→ Nike – empowerment, athleticism, overcoming adversity

- → Coca-Cola – happiness, togetherness, universal appeal
- → Dove – real beauty, body positivity, self-esteem
- → Patagonia – environmentalism, sustainability, responsibility
- → IKEA – practicality, affordability, family-centred living
- → Airbnb – belonging, community, authentic experiences
- → Spotify – personalisation, connection through music, data-driven insights
- → Amazon – customer-centricity, convenience, innovation
- → Google – innovation, accessibility, knowledge sharing.

The following is a list of skills and competencies that can form a framework for effective communication:

- → **Clarity:** the message should be clear and easily understood by the receiver. Avoid ambiguity, jargon and unnecessary complexity.
- → **Conciseness:** be brief and to the point without leaving out important information.
- → **Empathy:** understanding and sharing the feelings of another person.
- → **Adaptability:** tailoring the communication style to fit the audience, context and medium.
- → **Non-verbal communication:** be mindful of body language, facial expressions, gestures, eye contact and tone of voice.
- → **Feedback:** providing constructive responses and clar-

- → **Emotional intelligence:** being aware of your own emotions and the emotions of others.
- → **Consistency:** keeping messages and communication aligned across different mediums and contexts.
- → **Timing:** delivering the message at the appropriate time.
- → **Credibility:** the message should be pertinent to the recipients' interests, needs or concerns.
- → **Trustworthy**: the trustworthiness and authority of the communicator.
- → **Open-mindedness:** being open to new ideas, feedback and different perspectives during communication.
- → **Cultural awareness:** understanding the nuances and values of those from diverse cultures in order to communicate more effectively.
- → **Visual communication:** using visuals such as charts, infographics or slides to support and clarify the message.

Closer to home

While working in the London pub sector with an area manager whom I'll call Michael Brennan (not his real name – see also Chapter 9), I experienced ineffective communication and its negative impact. Michael was tasked with the business development of around 14 pubs.

I was managing one of the pubs in Blackheath, a leafy urban village in south-east London. I'd been there for four years, creating annual sales growth, and the previous year had achieved the best sales budget in the group of more than 100 pubs.

My experience of the area managers I'd worked with up to that point had been positive, as their communication skills measured well against the desired criteria and contributed to the success of the business at that time. I was clear in my communication as I felt safe to discuss any issues of concern and request what I needed. In return, I felt that they were clear about what was expected from the pub as a business. If we needed to clarify anything, we simply picked up the phone and had a quick chat before coming to a reasonable consensus on what action to take. On a monthly basis, the area manager would spend half a day going through figures, which were often presented as graphs, showing sales, profit, stock management, wages, costs, etc. The method used by the area managers was to start by discussing where things were going well, then spend time on items that could be improved and where help was needed before finishing on a strong performance example and formulating an action plan for the month ahead.

Michael joined the firm having not been directly involved in business development. While this wasn't a concern for the 14 managers he'd be overseeing, it appeared to be an issue for Michael, who seemed overwhelmed by the role and its responsibilities and got off to a difficult start. He was seldom clear in his communication and was inconsistent with it. It wasn't unusual for him to call on a Monday to discuss the weekly figures and offer a few words of encouragement, only to be in touch again by Wednesday, highly critical of something that had been discussed previously. This resulted in a lack of trust and failed attempts to build a positive relationship. I can recall occasions when I needed guidance on a compliance matter, when Michael would listen to the issue and the reason for my request but often interrupted and suggested it wasn't required at the time. If persuaded to take another look, he'd promise to come back to the discussion with more information, but I found that these were often empty promises.

Michael's communication skills were poor but I was disappointed in my response, too. I slowed down my communications with him to a needs-must basis. I'd often call another area manager with whom I'd established a good connection through the years, or call the head office directly. It was clear that Michael was upset by this but showed this through his body language; he didn't verbalise his unhappiness. I can now see my part in making the situation worse, but at the time I'd lost respect and had little desire to have a difficult conversation, nor did I feel it would have a positive result. I wasn't alone here and several other managers in the district were having similar issues with the area manager and his communication. I added this to my armour of justification and stumbled through months of decreased motivation and focus on my work. Our weekly call became nothing more than functional, with elements of tetchiness as we were both building trenches.

A new managing director intervened and his suggestion that we should 'lock ourselves in a padded room and not come out until we had sorted it' never materialised. With hindsight, one or indeed both of us should've called this much earlier and made a concerted effort to understand each other. A month later, after just over five years with the company, I resigned. Maybe my difficulty with Michael's communication style was a test of my commitment to the company, but my feeling was that the job had run its course. It wasn't exactly a knee-jerk reaction but my inability to connect with someone who was crucial to the success of my role made it too difficult for me to continue.

That was more than two decades ago and, in hindsight, I learned much from that 12-month period of my career. Michael's communication style was outside my control, but I could have changed my reactions and responses. He was a good teacher and I was a curious pupil, even if neither of us were conscious of those roles at the time. We both lacked vital human skills in our poor attempts at communication. Nowhere in our interactions did we use the human skills of collaboration, empathy, compassion, accountability or dealing with ambiguity that could've improved the outcomes for both us and the company. If the opposite of how Michael communicated was good, then now I'd do the opposite of his style, but more importantly find my own way of communicating. I'd also look at my part in this communication breakdown and clean my own side of the street.

Musings from Madonna's Caravan

In more recent years, I've become conscious of the fact that we never know what others are going through in their lives. Much of this awareness stems from my journey and battles with mental health at various levels of impact. Every day, we're turning up to work and our communities with insecurities. The principles of effective communication are a good guide but it's important to remember that the flight plan isn't always the flight path. The boxer Mike Tyson once famously observed that 'everyone has a plan until they get punched in the face'. Communication is a lifelong journey of improvement. There needs to be a greater emphasis on it within education and as a learning companion. Perhaps that's where compassion comes in. Do we show enough compassion when communication falls short of the standard expected? Do we allow space for the other person to be wrong occasionally? Compassion is not the absence of honesty; it's showing enough respect and courage to have difficult conversations as a way to manage effective communication.

Chapter 13

Vision and values

A compelling vision is succinct and paints a clear picture of the 'why' behind an organisation's existence and aims. For individuals, too, vision can help steer you towards an end goal. Values play a crucial role in vision as they're guiding principles, the scaffolding that helps to inform decision making and behaviour. I could mention the vision statements of Nike, Apple or Spotify but instead I'd like to share one more native to the soil of Ireland.

Early in 2020, at the start of the Covid-19 pandemic, I began working with a credit union in Loughrea, Galway, to help improve its vision. The Naomh Breandan Credit Union was performing well and the growth of its loan book was steady, if unspectacular. Along with a team of 12, we facilitated four workshops, carving out a vision from the organisation's objectives. It was important to involve the core team of staff to enable them to feel part of the process and thereby create a sense of ownership of the roadmap for the organisation's future. The following vision was created: 'Building a better tomorrow for all our community'. Some may say it's a simple phrase but these eight words succinctly encapsulate the mental picture that Naomh Breandan Credit Union wants to create in the minds of those it wishes to attract as members. The 'better tomorrow' suggests the hope and aspiration of many members who wish to improve their lives and that of their families. 'All our community' refers to a changing demographic, which now includes more than 50 nationalities living as citizens in the local community. By helping to build a better tomorrow for all the community, Naomh Breandan Credit Union staff are clear that their workplace values must align with the vision they created and agreed to.

Examples of some basic values are as follows:

→ integrity
→ innovation
→ passion
→ curiosity
→ learning and development
→ teamwork
→ accountability
→ respect
→ humility.

Increasingly, I'm seeing trends emerging that are paving the way for a new era of business that has values around the following:

→ diversity, equality and inclusion
→ transparency

→ sustainability

→ employee wellbeing

→ social impact and corporate social responsibility

→ ethical business practices.

It's important to note that a company vision statement with matching values is best achieved by involving as many people in the organisation as is logistically possible. If the task is outsourced and designed by a marketing or branding team, or even in-house by a small number of company executives and then 'imposed' upon the team of people expected to drive it forward, in my experience it loses credibility. Certainly, a strong leader can set the vision, or the 'why', but at the very least there should be discussion and agreement about values that will provide a meaningful pathway to get there.

Closer to home

On Saturday 12 June 2010, and along with many Donegal GAA football fans, I walked back to the car in Crossmaglen, Northern Ireland, saddened by the heavy defeat of our county team at the hands of the hosts, Armagh. It was a nine-point defeat but, in truth, a humiliation. The aftermath and post-mortem talk that occurs after such sporting annihilations is normally quite negative and depressing, and as we crawled out of the town of Crossmaglen, listening to the post-match interviews on the radio, it felt as if it would be years before we'd see our beloved Donegal mount anything close to a challenge to win an All-Ireland title, something that had only been achieved once before,

18 years previously in 1992. By the time we'd driven into Donegal, maybe two hours or so after the final whistle, our disappointment was replaced by the realisation that our footballing talent was as low as we'd seen in recent years.

To predict that a team of 12 players who endured such humiliation would be crowned All-Ireland champions two years later and recognised as the best team in Ireland would, at that moment, have been considered pie-in-the-sky talk. No one in our vast county would've believed it. But they hadn't considered one important factor: Jim McGuinness. The former player was part of a historic panel that had won the All-Ireland for the first time for Donegal in 1992. He fell into coaching and team management with his own club, Naomh Conaill, in West Donegal, and was pivotal in the club securing their first ever county titles in 2005 and 2010. He took an unorthodox route into education and sports science, studying many motivational sporting coaches, particularly Vince Lombardi, the US football icon. Also, in 2010, McGuinness managed the Donegal Under 21 side and brought them to an All-Ireland final against Dublin, narrowly losing out when a last-minute penalty hit the bar. He'd applied for the role of Donegal senior manager on two occasions prior to 2010 and suffered quite negative experiences of the process. His 'third coming' was different, however, and involved a different mindset and focus, which started in a hotel in the coastal village of Downings. In that hotel, McGuinness met each of the players he'd invited along and told them he'd help them win an All-Ireland within three years. Using the image of the houses that all the players could see from the window of the room they were sitting in, McGuinness focused their minds on one thing: the impact that an All-Ireland win would have on the people living in those houses and in homes all over Donegal.

This meeting was held a matter of months after the heavy disappointment in Armagh and significantly the majority of players present were part of the defeated squad, yet here was the new manager setting out an ambitious objective of reaching the pinnacle of their sporting career. In creating a clear vision to win an All-Ireland within three years for the benefit of all the supporters and people of the county, he motivated and compelled the players to think about each and every person in Donegal, establishing a powerful narrative in their minds and hearts around why winning mattered.

The values were never written or stated but that doesn't mean they weren't there. Commitment was certainly a required value. McGuinness knew that a dramatic uplift in physical conditioning was necessary and only those who were fully committed were likely to survive the core strength and conditioning demands he was going to put on them. If winning an All-Ireland was the goal, dedication to training, improving skills and supporting teammates was the price to be paid. Trust and integrity were another pair of values that were non-negotiable in McGuinness's vision. He needed to be trusted by his players and backroom team and the players had to be fully honest within the squad, so that integrity was protected.

Tactically, McGuinness and his staff brought in an innovative if highly controversial strategy of play. Although much more complex in practice than my description here, the Donegal team under McGuinness in that first year was set up technically as one that was extremely difficult to score against. A high-energy defensive formation saw all 15 players defend with a high intensity matched by physical strength, a tactic that suffocated teams accustomed to more open play. The games in that initial season were based on this approach, minimising the opposition's score and then doing just enough to win. TV commentators and observers weren't over the moon about the style but McGuinness, the players and 95 per cent of us in Donegal weren't too concerned, as we won our way to victory in an Ulster Championship for the first time in 19 years. Victory and success were not the result of an explosion of new talent but the creation of a compelling vision with values that were shared by all.

Innovation was required in this sporting project and as a value, it requires a safe place for mistakes and experimentation. The training sessions under McGuinness were such a place. The psychological safety required for the innovative approach of high-intensity defending and braking at speed was present. There was room for players to get it wrong at training. Judgement and criticism were replaced by players figuring out a better way of doing things, all with the goal of winning an All-Ireland. Leaders emerged in the team and McGuinness oversaw a dramatic change in performance in his first year before a two-point defeat by an extremely talented Dublin side in the semi-final and in one of the most controversial games in years, pairing Dublin's free-flowing and attacking style against the opposite approach by Donegal. Dublin only scored two points in the opening half and the half-time score of 0–4 to 0–2 was the lowest-ever score recorded in senior championship football. This was certainly not for the purists or those waiting to be entertained. McGuinness promised an All-Ireland and explained the reason why. He never promised how or what he'd do to achieve it. It's said that if the vision is strong enough, the rest will follow. His vision and that of the players were so strong that the strategy would be realised regardless of the opinion of others.

The following year would see even more improvement and growth in the structures and vision. The values set down at the outset, although not written on the walls of the dressing room, were certainly in the walls and were pushed further. Donegal had now come within two points of a Dublin side that would go on to dominate Gaelic football for several years. In 2012, a year after Jim McGuinness had set the vision and got others to buy into it, an increase in physical conditioning was seen with another layer of strength and speed introduced. Tactically, the same strategy would have to vary as other teams would analyse the Donegal of the previous year. Innovation was key. McGuinness placed an even greater importance on integrity, which included keeping everything that happened at camp in the camp. This was tested when an integral player, Kevin Cassidy, contributed to a book in which McGuinness perceived him to have broken a code of silence. The result was a highly publicised fallout and the exit of Cassidy from the squad. There are varying perceptions about this, but it did highlight the strength McGuinness placed on the values he held as integral to the vision of winning an All-Ireland.

Donegal went on to win the All-Ireland in 2012. The vision was to win an All-Ireland within three years for the people of Donegal and this was achieved in the second year. Players, backroom staff and management had brought about the near-impossible task of turning around a devastating sporting defeat into the supreme Gaelic football achievement, all within 18 months.

The social impact and economic benefits of winning an All-Ireland can never be underestimated. Role models emerge along with systems and approaches that inspire change in business as well as sport. The importance of setting a clear and compelling vision was played out in front of our eyes. McGuinness did more than win an All-Ireland. He handed us a template for how vision and values work and their importance in all aspects of life. It's difficult to measure the economic and social impact that this victory had on our county but most would agree it was significant.

Musings from Madonna's Caravan

Like most people, I haven't always considered vision to be important. It was never covered in my education, although it should have been. I wandered into different positions and my performance varied from being completely inadequate to being OK, and on occasion doing well, when I started to understand and appreciate team dynamics. In recent years, I've been better at seeing the importance of vision, establishing the 'why' and identifying the values required for the 'how'. My knowledge has come from reading and listening to podcasts and TED talks such as Sir Ken Robinson's 'Do schools kill creativity?' and Simon Sinek's 'How great leaders inspire action'. When the vision is clear, the strategy is easier. This book is part of a vision. That vision is to establish a Human Skills Institute. The values needed to get there are to be as authentic and honest as possible, but not to the detriment of others.

Chapter 14

Stress management

Stress isn't completely avoidable, nor is it always bad. When it's short term and channelled positively, it can lead to growth, action and change. Stress management refers to a set of practices that help us cope with and reduce the negative effects of stress in our lives. The goal is to maintain a healthy balance between life's demands and our ability to cope with them, preventing stress from becoming overwhelming and harmful, or even fatal. From the research I've done as a result of my own experience with a dangerous level of stress, recognising the sources of tension, whether work-related, personal or emotional, is the first step to managing it.

My personal journey with unmanaged stress, which led to a heart attack several years ago, created a desire in me to provide people with the tools to recognise the signs of overwhelm and burnout and the techniques to find a sense of balance in their lives. When unmanaged, long-term stress can take a costly toll on the body, contributing to high blood pressure, increased cholesterol levels and inflammation, all of which raise the risk of stroke, heart disease and heart attacks. It can also have an impact on mental health, leading to anxiety or depression.

In 2021, I began open-water sea swimming with a wholehearted and drama-free group of people, and the benefits have been immense. Sea swimming enables me to practise stress-management techniques such as deep breathing and mindfulness, building exercise into my life in ways that feel natural and easy. Practices such as yoga, meditation, progressive muscle relaxation and spending time in nature can also significantly reduce stress levels. I find sea swimming therapeutic and energising as there are fewer things as raw and close to nature than being exposed to the conditions of the open sea in all seasons. It's also a source of social support, which has been proven to reduce anxiety and improve resilience. I'm also blessed with strong family support, led by my wife, Toni. I also have supportive co-workers and valued friends, and can't emphasise enough the importance of these relationships in maintaining both good mental and physical health. Not everyone is able to find strength through relationships with family or friends and many will use alcohol, drugs, pornography and/or gambling as a way to cope with stressful situations.

My journey with alcoholism didn't begin because I was looking for ways to relax or unwind. Nevertheless, I experienced feelings of relief when I drank, so I can identify with people who turn to alcohol, drugs or indeed other behaviours such as pornography or gambling to cope with stress. If you want to develop healthier coping mechanisms and improve overall wellbeing, it's crucial to understand the relationship between these behaviours and managing stress. Addressing both stress management and addictive behaviours with a counsellor or in therapy can be beneficial. I availed myself of therapy following my heart attack and found it very helpful.

With the evolving demands of modern life and the rapid pace of change the world continues to experience, the need for therapy and/or other outlets to manage stress is only going to increase. It's therefore of vital importance that workplaces have the tools to help staff identify and manage stress, whether that's within the workplace or outside it. Organisations that prioritise stress management support create a foundation for long-term success because healthier and happier employees will be more engaged, productive and committed. Caring for employees' wellbeing isn't just morally right; it's a strategic advantage that benefits both individuals and organisations.

Closer to home

At 8.30 am on 5 July 2018, I was taken into theatre at Galway University Hospital for what was initially meant to be double bypass heart surgery. This was six weeks after I'd suffered a heart attack, in a manner that was very different to how I'd seen it depicted in the movies. On that day in May, I was delivering training to a group of supervisors from local development projects in south-east Donegal. Before lunchtime, I felt a sensation in my chest and a lesser sensation in my left arm. Although I knew that these might be signs of a heart issue, there was no pain, so I rattled on with the class. During a group breakout session, I used the heart rate monitor on my phone to find it measuring my heart at 130 beats per minute.

Within a couple of hours I was in my doctor's surgery, being informed that I'd suffered a heart attack and would need to be taken to hospital in an ambulance. In short, four arteries leading to the heart, including the artery referred to as the 'widow maker', were dangerously blocked. The nickname is given to this artery because it can lead to a massive heart attack, which is often fatal if not treated immediately.

The day before the quadruple bypass surgery, one of the consultants asked me a series of questions about lifestyle, work and stress, and although initially reluctant to offer up his opinion on the factors that led to the heart attack, he conceded that it was most likely stress related. This was a huge surprise to me. I didn't see myself as stressed, and yet the questions he asked in his investigation and the answers I offered suggested that stress had indeed resulted in me having life-saving surgery at the age of 56.

In the days after the surgery, which by all accounts was successful, I was a sponge for information from the care team as to how best to recover from the operation and reduce my chances of visiting them again. They expressed the importance of walking and, before I was discharged, I had to show that I could walk 400 metres along the corridor. Back home, I gradually increased the distance every day, and 500 metres turned into a kilometre, increasing to two kilometres, and with it came a boost in confidence and feelings of gratitude. Soon, I was walking 5 km four times a week. By the following year, along with a colleague, I walked 110 km over five days along an old railway line from one side of Donegal to the other. This was a huge milestone, not just in terms of my physical recovery but also in my challenge of coping with stress. In that year, I made it a priority to build this positive behaviour into my routine, and the benefits were vast.

Musings from Madonna's Caravan

I've long been aware of the impact of alcoholism in my native area of Donegal. It's by no means just an Irish problem. According to data on global alcohol consumption from the World Health Organization, an estimated 400 million people aged 15 years and older live with alcohol use disorders, and an estimated 209 million live with alcohol dependence. There's a distinct relationship between stress and alcohol consumption, and my observations and personal battle with the disease of alcoholism point to a much bigger familial problem than many would care to admit. Addiction of any kind frequently signals deeper emotional, psychological or environmental problems. Although alcohol has largely been the traditional drug of choice due to its acceptance in society, we're faced with the growing use of recreational drugs. Because of its availability online, gambling has seen greater numbers of people present to treatment centres, often in serious debt. From anecdotal observations in my local area, I'd say that a significant percentage of homes are impacted by problems due to alcohol, gambling or drugs.

In addition, smartphone use is a growing area of concern, as it can contribute to greater levels of stress for many reasons. Instant gratification from scrolling endless content can encourage repeated use, while social media can contribute to feelings of anxiety, depression and loneliness. There's strong evidence to show a correlation between the emergence of smartphones and the declining state of mental health in children and teenagers in the years 2010–2014 (Haidt 2024).

Admittedly, my own smartphone use is often unhealthy. I can access my emails, all social media platforms and receive messages at all hours of the day. I operate so much of my life via my phone and, while it can be efficient, it becomes problematic when I'm at home and in the presence of my family. The use of smartphones is certainly something we must include in the human skill of stress management, or it risks becoming normalised and damaging.

Chapter 15

Empathy

Empathy enables individuals to be socially aware and in doing so helps them to develop and maintain functioning relationships. Empathy is about using your imagination to step into another's shoes, to try to understand what they're experiencing. An individual who practises empathy will often show an interest in the concerns of others, identifying verbal and non-verbal emotional signals. Empathetic skills allow a deep understanding of colleagues, customer needs and an awareness of the environmental, social and governmental impact of an organisation. At some level, empathy comes naturally to most people, but it's a skill that can be developed and often improves with practice and experience. The workplace and society can benefit greatly from understanding and practising empathy.

These are the elements of empathy:

→ **Inquisitiveness** involves being curious about the environment in which you find yourself, listening to other viewpoints and using them to increase your understanding of a particular topic. It's the ability to ask questions, actively listen to diverse audiences and think creatively. Inquisitiveness supports inclusiveness and a continual learning process that aids your ability to understand other perspectives.

→ **Mindful listening** is the ability to truly understand and interpret what's being said. Often, you may simply respond without paying attention, leading to misinterpretation or leaving the other person feeling that their words aren't valued. Being able to do this well can enhance interactions and relationships, leading to more meaningful and productive outcomes. Listening also includes non-verbal cues such as eye contact, an open body posture and moving the head in agreement.

→ **Cognisance** is the ability to be truthful with yourself and aware of how your emotions impact the people around you. Being cognisant enables you to take responsibility for your own actions and learn from mistakes. Being aware of how your beliefs, values and behaviours impact others enables you to be considerate to others. For example, being aware of an area you're not an expert in and engaging with someone who is will lead to the development of both parties.

→ **Emotional intelligence** through the understanding of verbal and non-verbal communication skills will allow you to understand the feelings or emotional state of others. Being able to analyse how others feel will enable you to provide support to another's wellbeing. Furthermore, it will give you a deeper level of understanding of others, leading to more effective relationships through acknowledgement of their beliefs, values and behaviours. I like the idea that emotional intelligence is now up there with cognitive intelligence as a measure of someone's worth. I know many 'intelligent' people who lack emotional intelligence, and as such find it difficult to leverage their intelligence in the workplace. (See Chapter 7 for more about EQ.)

→ **Open-mindedness** refers to the ability to actively listen and comprehend other points of view that may differ from your own, to give space and understand another perspective in order to productively engage with others. Other views may trigger more creative solutions to a particular scenario, or they may not. Either way, you're demonstrating an ability to see something from someone else's perspective.

There's some evidence suggesting that people may be becoming less empathetic, though the reasons and implications are complex. Studies have shown a decline in empathy in younger generations over the past few decades. For example, research on college students has suggested that empathy levels have decreased significantly since the 1980s, particularly since 2000. To better understand this decline, we should try to understand why it's happening.

→ **Digital and social media:** the rise of social media and digital communication has changed how people interact. These platforms can often create shallow connections, a culture of comparison, less face-to-face interaction and therefore a reduction in emotional exchanges.

→ **Cultural shifts:** in my experience, an increasing focus on individual self-promotion, often amplified by social media, has contributed to a decline in genuine empathy. The rewards for self-publicity and visibility offered by digital platforms can lead individuals to prioritise showcasing their achievements, appearance or lifestyle over compassion and connecting authentically with others.

→ **Media exposure:** constant exposure to negative news, violence and large-scale suffering can desensitise people, leading to a form of 'compassion fatigue' where individuals feel overwhelmed and unable to respond emotionally to suffering. The birth and subsequent explosion of the smartphone are linked to an increase in anxiety in younger generations. Jonathan Haidt's 2024 bestseller, *The Anxious Generation*, provides a revealing insight into this problem.

→ **Economic pressures:** rising economic inequality and financial stress can also shift focus inward. When individuals are focused on basics such as having a home, food, safety, relationships and survival, they may find it harder to empathise with others. This social gap can add to a decline in empathy.

It's my belief that empathy should be taught as a key human skill at all levels of education and in the workplace.

Closer to home

West Donegal, where I live and work, is a four-and-a-half-hour drive from Dublin and a four-hour drive from Galway, both cities that host our main cancer services. In recent years, there have been limited services available in Donegal and neighbouring Derry as part of a cross-border collaboration. However, most of the cancer-related services involve an arduous and tiresome drive. For cancer patients or indeed patients receiving any treatment, this can be an overwhelming experience by public bus.

Mary Coyle is the manager of a local community centre in the Donegal Gaeltacht, an Irish-speaking area that's one of the most populated rural areas in Europe. Among the many services this community centre provides is accompanied cancer flights from the local regional airport in West Donegal to Dublin airport. Those needing to attend a Dublin hospital for cancer diagnosis, operations and treatment can avail themselves of subsidised flights for €20 return and a carer can buy the return for €40. This has been and continues to be a great service that's funded mainly by local people running events.

Mary and her hard-working, compassionate team at Ionad Naomh Padraig (St Patrick's Centre) took over the coordination of the flights quite a few years back. They listened carefully to the needs of the cancer patients and their families. They observed first hand the challenges they faced. Very soon, the local community centre began a car transfer service for patients, driven by local volunteers, to Galway, which isn't served by an air or train link. This allowed cancer patients to be driven in comfort to their consultation or treatment and back home again. The volunteer drivers acted as carers for the trip, and this greatly added to the service. Often, the drivers would spend hours alone with the cancer patients and could identify other issues they encountered. This would be fed back in confidence to Mary as the centre manager. She observed and listened to what was happening within her community. She could see that, although the transporting of cancer patients was much improved, there was also the psychological strain of fear, job insecurity, financial pressure and overwhelm. The community centre team created counselling services in a safe and comfortable room within the building, where not only the cancer patient but also their family and friends could come and talk about how they were coping with the patient's ongoing cancer journey. This service is now available three times a week and is being used regularly.

This wouldn't be possible without the compassion and empathy that's necessary to ensure that the services being provided are the ones that the patients and community need. Mary doesn't assume what they want, and removes the guesswork by continually observing, listening and asking the important questions. The service is partly funded by central government but a large amount of the money is raised locally by community activities, charity events, swims, tractor runs, 5 km walks, etc.

I became involved in an annual 2 km swim, which raises around €15,000 annually for the cancer flights. The positive feeling of helping others is a personal benefit. What motivates me to swim throughout the year is taking part in the cancer flight swim in August. That has both physical and emotional value to me. There are about 30 of us who do that. This is social and community empathy – listening to a real problem, not assuming but asking those impacted how best they can be helped, and then acting on that.

Empathy is about listening to learn and learning to listen. It's about hearing and feeling what's being said, observing, and if you don't believe what you hear, then believe what you see. The success of the cancer flights as a service is based on the human skill of empathy.

Musings from Madonna's Caravan

We often look for inspiration in academic writings, books, movies or stories that take place in other countries or continents. I was guilty of this and would often see achievements elsewhere as brilliant or inspiring. Having spent 13 great years in the London area, I returned to West Donegal feeling so much more appreciative of local people who exhibit outstanding traits. In general, the people of the area are resilient and there's a tradition of helping others in need. Through study, I gained a whole new level of appreciation for local leaders because I could see that the people in my own community have the many human skills required by leaders, including empathy.

Empathy has been a weak area for me, but it's a skill that I must continue practising diligently and with focus. I've always been too quick to speak and less good at listening. I've failed to listen properly to what's being said and instead overthink what I'm going to say when the other person stops talking so that my story can be validated. This damages the ability to truly hear and listen to what's being said. Being aware of this and accepting the deficit is a start, and embracing empathy is the journey.

Chapter 16

Compassion

I believe that compassion is an essential human skill that can enable employees to feel secure, respected and valued, leading to higher workplace engagement and performance. In 2024, a survey carried out by my company found that 95 per cent of people felt compassion was either crucially important (70 per cent) or very important (25 per cent) in a business sense.

    I see compassion as incredibly important both in life and in business, as it's essential for forming meaningful connections and building trust. In business, strong relationships with customers, employees and stakeholders are the foundations of success. During my work with companies, I've also witnessed first hand how compassion fosters an environment where collaboration thrives. When individuals feel valued and understood, they're more likely to work together effectively, which is crucial in any team dynamic. Even when conflict arises, as it inevitably does, compassion is a vital cog in the wheel of constructive conflict resolution, encouraging individuals to listen, empathise and seek solutions that consider everyone's perspectives and needs. These are essential components of any company or organisational culture.

The World Health Organization and International Labour Organisation's 2022 report on mental health at work cited that depression and anxiety cause significant losses in productivity globally, highlighting the need for supportive and inclusive work cultures. For businesses looking to improve their customer experience, displaying compassion towards customers is crucial for loyalty and satisfaction. Understanding customers' needs and challenges allows companies to tailor their offerings and services more effectively. Technology will, of course, speed up efficiency and the ability to scale service, accelerating unprecedented growth rates in many businesses. But while technology can be viewed as an enhancement of the human touch, it cannot replace it. Compassion can't be digitised. It can, however, be taught. Some people may naturally exhibit more compassionate behaviour but for those who don't, compassion can be cultivated. It's a skill that can be developed and strengthened through various practices and approaches.

So, how do we create a more compassionate world? This is an important question for us all. It might be expected that compassion for others starts with compassion for ourselves, but might that be seen as self-indulgent? There's no guarantee that people who are self-compassionate are more compassionate towards others and neither is there enough evidence to suggest that those who exhibit compassion are themselves self-compassionate. Many will argue that you can't pour from an empty vessel and that to give compassion, you must have a level of balance and stability in your own life.

There are many kinds and shades of compassion. The term 'idiotic compassion' is where a family member, friend, work colleague accepts the story being told to them and offers immediate and ongoing support to the person outlining the issue they're experiencing, prioritising a desire to avoid discomfort and enabling unhealthy behaviours. This kind of compassion can be damaging on many fronts. In the context of the drama triangle (Karpman 1968), a well-researched theory that consists of a perpetrator, a victim and a rescuer who each contribute to a negative triangle of drama, it can be explained as the persecutor harshly criticising the victim, making them feel powerless; then the rescuer, driven by misplaced empathy, steps in to comfort the victim without addressing the role of the persecutor. Too often, relationships are damaged rather than repaired or sustained by this form of compassion, where people convince themselves that they're acting compassionately yet are doing the opposite. Once you discover this negative form of compassion, you have a responsibility to explore it further, act as a leader and, at the very least, not take part in the activity yet also be prepared to highlight its implications and consequences.

True compassion involves actions and attitudes that genuinely prioritise the wellbeing of others. It must be authentic and often unscripted. Its main elements include empathy and active listening, recognition and appreciation, flexibility and understanding, fair and ethical treatment and support during crises, yet it should always feature constructive feedback and honesty. When this balance is achieved, great things tend to happen to those offering compassion and those receiving it.

Closer to home

On a Monday in July 2024, I received a message via Facebook from my cousin, Stephen Boyle, who lives in New York. Stephen often messages and, at first, I thought it might be a comment about Donegal's narrow defeat to Galway in a Gaelic football match in Dublin the previous day. I was going to leave it but there was a picture attached and I recognised the person, so I opened the message. It was Stephen telling me that his brother's daughter, Chloe, had died suddenly. Chloe was 17, living on Long Island, New York, and had become unwell while working her summer job in a restaurant. She went to the staff bathroom and, when she didn't return, staff members went to check and found her collapsed on the floor. With her parents Tommy and Erina and brother Liam by her side in hospital, Chloe died of a bleed in the brain.

I felt compelled to travel to New York for the wake and funeral. My experience of death is that the support of family, friends and community provides an immeasurable comfort to those who are grieving. I flew into Boston, where two of my sons, Hugh and Dominic, live and work, and it was decided that we'd drive from Boston to New York together. As we made the four-hour journey from Massachusetts through Rhode Island, Connecticut and across the Throgs Neck Bridge and Long Island, although grateful to be accompanied by my sons, I wasn't looking forward to what I expected to be a very sad occasion. As we made our way into the funeral home, my immediate thought was that we were entering a theatre of compassion. The wake had begun 30 minutes before we arrived and already the line of sympathisers went out of the door. A police guard of honour was in place inside as a tribute and a mark of respect and support for Tommy, a former member, now retired, of the New York Police Department. Tommy's brothers were there with Erina and young Liam. Chloe had recently graduated from high school and was due to go to college in South Carolina that September. Many of her high school friends were there to pay their respects and offer condolences. I was imagining how very difficult this experience would've been for many of the teenagers but I could see that the practice of coming together in the funeral home allowed them time and space to talk to each other, hug each other, cry, laugh at past stories, be there together and process their loss in their own way. Their presence was also comforting for the family. Collectively they displayed a form of compassion towards each other and Chloe's family that was touching and, in many ways, inspirational.

Chloe's parents' generation, many of whom are the sons and daughters of those who emigrated from Ireland in the 1950s and 1960s, were also in attendance. Police officers, nurses, doctors, scaffolders, contractors, tradespeople, restaurant owners and publicans gathered among others with multinational origins to show their love and respect to the family and hold them with warmth and kind-heartedness at this devastating time. This was Long Island, but it had all the markings of a wake in Donegal. It was authentic and genuine and, for me, it embodied compassion. There was nothing staged or prepared because, for the tragic passing of a 17-year-old, nothing can be prepared. People attended because they felt they needed to be there. They either found words or just listened.

I sat with Chloe's 93-year-old grandfather, Hughie, my uncle, as he explained what had happened on the day leading up to Chloe's passing from this life into another. I was conscious that he wanted to tell this story and I needed to be present and not distracted by the many mourners passing in and out of the funeral home. I felt this was the most important thing I had to do during this sad trip. Perhaps in protecting Tommy, Erina, Liam and his own immediate family, he hadn't yet told his story of the day. Hughie is from a generation of tough Donegal tunnel men, for whom emotion, or at least showing it, wouldn't have been natural. As he talked about his experience of the tragedy, stopping twice to compose himself, I felt I was in an extremely privileged yet responsible position. To hear him properly, I sat with my ear close to him. I didn't want to miss anything or lose any of his story. I had an overwhelming sense that I was meant to be there at that moment. Am I a natural listener? No! However, I've become aware of my tendency to become distracted, so I try to work consciously at improving this. I felt a sense of something strong as Hughie finished with a squeeze of my upper arm as a message that I read as 'Thank you'. We both stood up and I told him we were going back to Boston and would see him again on Tuesday for the funeral. We hugged and he thanked me 'for coming over like this'. We were both benefactors amid the tragedy.

I learned a valuable lesson about compassionate presence. At 62 years of age, I'm prepared to learn, unlearn and relearn. I felt gratified to be in a wake setting and yet couldn't help wondering if this was wrong. As my two sons and I left the funeral home, I could still feel the outpouring of compassion in the building. The atmosphere wasn't one of sadness alone; it was filled with empathy, understanding and support. Smiles, tears and laughter were interwoven with grief, yet with an overarching ray of compassion.

Two days later, at Chloe's funeral mass, I understood better why the wake at the funeral home was so compassionate. Chloe was extremely compassionate and especially to animals. She was a 'Swiftie' (a raving fan of Taylor Swift). This came across in the eulogy and the remarks by Tommy and Liam painted a personal, humorous and moving tribute to Chloe, a compassionate teenager.

Musings from Madonna's Caravan

In recent years, I've experienced the value of compassion as well as a better understanding of it. My serious heart event in 2018, which resulted in a quadruple bypass operation, sharply focused my attention on the here and now. The mantra 'Yesterday is history, tomorrow is a mystery and all we have is today' rang very true for me. My gratitude levels heightened after my hospitalisation and subsequent recovery. I'd been given another chance by a team of skilled physicians. Nurses and physiotherapists continued my care, which I found to be highly compassionate. After the operation and while recovering at home, there were times when I'd cry like a child while watching something sad or thought-provoking on Netflix. This brought me relief. It was new, cleansing, different. There were also darker days. I was warned about feelings of despair but the warning doesn't prepare you for it. The up-and-down battle was real. It's not over, but I'm now quite stable and I'm grateful for that.

The lessons in compassion that I experienced at young Chloe's wake and funeral in New York impacted me greatly. I witnessed the power of compassion. In business, the results of fostering greater compassion are just as positive. If the compassion in these examples is such a help, it would follow that compassion is an important human skill and one that's vital in the workplace. Compassion is required when difficult conversations are necessary or when hard decisions need to be taken. Allowing a poor standard to continue or allowing an important issue to remain unaddressed because we don't wish to upset someone is not compassion.

I also believe that self-compassion is important and culturally that has been my biggest challenge. In a business sense, compassion for customers is important. More important, and increasingly so, is compassion for the team at work. Compassion here is about caring for the team. Understanding what staff are going through and allowing them space and time to deal with issues outside work are now important factors as businesses move away from strict and regimental structures. As work–life balance becomes ever more important and indeed demanded, flexible work arrangements must be considered. By doing so, the team will reciprocate and show compassion to customers, and the outcome is increased alignment, harmony, loyalty, sales and sustainable profit. Compassion is now an important factor in workplace leadership.

Complete compassion is probably not something any individual or organisation can achieve, but we can at the very least be mindful of it and aspire towards it. Compassion is an action and not a word. You can think compassionately but it only works if you put it into practice. In life as in business, the need for compassion is evident and we should and can embrace that need. The world and its people are worth it.

Chapter 17

Creativity and design thinking

In March 2023, I headed to Boston for meetings at Massachusetts Institute of Technology. MIT has been ranked as the number one university in the world by QS World University Rankings for 12 straight years. My curiosity and hunger for information on the human skills research initiated by Professor George Westerman had brought me across the Atlantic to this centre of excellence and at the kind invitation of George, who has been a cheerleader since we first met. Not only was I afforded access to a great tour of MIT but also to plenty of information about the reasons why a world-leading institute of technology conducted a study of human skills. Why was there such a focus on human skills at a time when MIT should surely have been educating their US and international students to help them keep up with the ever-increasing pace of digital transformation?

Microsoft Research was founded just up the road from MIT in July 2008. The New England lab in Cambridge builds on Microsoft's commitment to collaborate with the broader research community and pursues new, interdisciplinary areas of research that bring together core computer scientists and social scientists to understand, model and enable computing and online experiences of the future. As part of their open collaboration, they would at times seek support from MIT in technical and digital engineering research.

The story goes that Microsoft felt that their 'techies' or 'digital geeks' (their words, not mine) were slowing down in their ability to keep up with the pace of innovation and change and, as such, there was a risk that, as a global leader in technology, Microsoft might fall behind. Microsoft also suspected that their tech people and brightest minds weren't falling behind due to lack of technical or engineering qualifications but from a lack of focus on the human skills required for large collaborative projects. The story continues that Microsoft made the short walk down the road to MIT and had a 'coffee' to discuss this assumption. Could MIT help with looking at which human skills were required by highly technical employees? And had I, simply by the nature of my curiosity and brashness in getting invited to MIT, walked into an interesting challenge in technology?

Ainslie Peters is a Canadian-born lecturer at Atlantic Technological University in Galway, teaching industrial and product design and design thinking process and principles. Ainslie is now employed as an effective programme manager with the newly opened CREW (Creative Enterprise West) innovation and enterprise hub for the creative design sector, where she helps entrepreneurs and start-ups in the digital creative industries to launch, grow and scale. During a visit to the impressive CREW building in 2024 with two of my colleagues, I explained the MIT trip to Ainslie as she showed us around the facility. Expecting a quick rebuttal, I offered a loose comment: 'It's said that 40 per cent of technical design thinking is empathy.' There was no rebuttal, but an addition by Ms Peters: 'Charlie, I would have no hesitation in going as far as to say that design thinking is 100 per cent empathy.' Even though I'd left MIT months earlier with strong evidence of the power of human skills, here was a leading force in design in Ireland with a strong belief that empathy was key to creativity and design thinking. (See Chapter 15 for more about the human skill of empathy.)

I could write the story of feeling overwhelmed by being in the presence of these brilliant leaders of education, George Westerman and Ainslie Peters. However, I had long held a view that education was contradictory in many respects. Why shouldn't I go inside the doors of the great centres of research and learning and ask for information? Education involves a lot of protectionism. Many insiders try hard to complicate it, to protect it from becoming more democratic and open to all. Some but not all universities need to demolish many of their ivory-tower symbolisms and ancient hierarchical structures. They are, in many ways, light years behind the more recent changes globally in ensuring that those who go through their courses are prepared for the future with the skills they require. Many universities prioritise research output over high-quality teaching. Professors are encouraged to publish academic papers, sometimes at the expense of their teaching duties, leading to large lecture sizes and a lack of personalised attention. The customer, aka the student, is often not the priority, and this is wrong. In recent years, students and employers have often noted that curricula are overly academic, leaving graduates without the hands-on skills required for real-world applications. Universities are often seen as inaccessible to marginalised groups due to financial, social and geographic barriers. Underrepresentation of women, ethnic minorities and students from lower socioeconomic backgrounds remains a problem in many regions.

Therefore, as much as I respect many involved in third-level education management and the many who challenge the system from within, I didn't feel at all underqualified to enter discussions about the absence of human skills education. I've found many inside the system of third-level education to be truly outstanding people pushing for the change that needs to happen. Each of them has a common trait, which is that they're equally committed to teaching their students in a compassionate way, yet frustrated that they can't always give the personalised attention required by the system. They've been great supporters of both my study of and research into human skills and the aspiration to create a Human Skills Institute in Donegal.

Closer to home

As a teenager, I was once stung by a bee or a wasp. I never asked them which they were. It was sore and sudden. I therefore never viewed it as an insect I was particularly

Creativity and design thinking

fond of. Last year, my beloved wife Toni was showing me some flowers she'd purchased for the garden. She told me she'd bought extra lavender because it was good for the bees and they liked the colour because they could see it the best. She explained that local shops were selling 'bee-friendly' flowers. Toni also explained that if she'd seen a bee that was struggling, she'd put out a bowl of sugared water and that the bee would indulge and then fly off, fuelled up after its exhaustion.

I felt slightly guilty about my unconscious bias towards bees. I decided to be more open to hearing about them and so Toni, seizing the opportunity, gradually brought me more information to the point where I was becoming interested in the swarm mentality or, as it has become known, the group intelligence of bees – their creativity and design thinking. I started to become slightly more interested in watching bees in the back garden extracting nectar with their snout and pollen with their back legs and then returning to their hive, which I could never see.

Then, in 2024, the well-known workplace consultant and author Siobhán McHale, originally from Galway, published *The Hive Mind at Work*. It's her latest in a series of books about workplace culture based on the hive mindset of bees, which she has studied. In the human workplace, traditional approaches to design thinking fall into one of two categories. Organisations either function like machines, where managers pull change levers to 'fix' problems with an engineer's mindset (IQ), or people form social networks wherein individual influencers make change happen by developing effective interpersonal relationships (EQ). Both have limited success. According to Siobhan, there's a third option. Organisations are complex ecosystems that require a hive mind or group intelligence (GQ) to bring about meaningful and lasting change.

We can learn a lot about creativity and design thinking from bees and their hive mindset. The way in which bees operate within a hive demonstrates a fascinating blend of collective intelligence, innovation and adaptability, which can inspire human approaches to creativity and problem solving. This is partly being played out in my back garden in West Donegal, yet I was oblivious to it because of a bee (or possibly a wasp) sting 45 years ago. It's a great lesson in looking at nature for the answer to our human problems. Here are a few key lessons from bees that align with creativity and design thinking principles, as discussed in *The Hive Mind at Work* as well as conversations I've had with a local beekeeper near to my home.

1. Collaborative innovation

Bees work collectively to achieve a shared goal, much like the collaborative nature of design thinking. Bees rely on group communication (such as the waggle dance to signal the location of food sources) and collective decision making. This mirrors how creativity often thrives when diverse teams come together to brainstorm, test ideas and iterate solutions. Design thinking emphasises collaboration, where interdisciplinary teams bring different perspectives to address challenges. Like the hive's collective intelligence, a design thinking team pools ideas, critiques them and arrives at more innovative solutions than any one person might have alone.

2. Iterative problem solving

Bees are constantly adapting to their environment. If a nectar source dries up, they scout for new ones. They experiment, adapt and refine their strategies. This reflects the iterative nature of design thinking, which encourages prototyping, testing and refining solutions until the best outcome is found. The hive mind is flexible and continuously evolving, just as design thinking thrives on iteration. Mistakes and failures are seen as valuable insights, helping to shape the next steps toward a better solution.

3. User-centred design (nature-centred in bees)

Beehives are designed with distinct zones for different purposes – for example, a brood zone near the hive's core for warmth and protection of the eggs; honey storage in outer areas that provides insulation; and pollen storage near the brood zone for easy feeding of the young bees. Workers also fan their wings at the hive entrance to maintain airflow. Similarly, in design thinking, we focus on solving problems from the user's perspective by creating solutions that are efficient, functional and elegant.

4. Communication and feedback loops

Bees use their communication channels effectively through waggle dances to guide the hive. They communicate information about food sources, threats or necessary changes to the hive. This feedback loop keeps the hive agile and responsive. In design thinking, continual feedback from stakeholders, users or team members helps to refine ideas and improve the design process. Just like bees, effective communication within teams or with end users ensures that the final product is useful and relevant. When Ainslie Peters told me that design thinking was 100 per cent empathy, she was overscoring it for emphasis, but the bees do listen intently to the communication coming from the other bees in the group.

5. Simplicity and efficiency in design

Bees create solutions that aren't overly complex but highly efficient, such as the structure of honeycombs. The hexagonal shape is a natural optimisation of space and resources, achieving the greatest structural integrity with the least amount of material.

In creativity and design thinking, the best solutions are often the simplest. The goal is not to overcomplicate but to streamline and deliver solutions that meet user needs efficiently, much like bees do when building their hive.

6. Resilience and adaptability

Bees exhibit remarkable resilience. When faced with environmental changes or threats, they adjust their behaviour to ensure the survival of the hive. This adaptability is crucial for problem solving in design thinking, where unexpected challenges often arise. Creativity requires flexibility, and the hive mindset teaches us to pivot and find new approaches when necessary, which is an essential aspect of both creativity and innovation.

7. Sustainability and resource management

Bees are masters of sustainability, carefully managing their resources (nectar, pollen and honey) to ensure the long-term survival of the hive. This thoughtful use of resources can inspire creative solutions that are environmentally and socially sustainable. In design thinking, resource constraints often lead to more innovative, sustainable and ethical solutions.

Musings from Madonna's Caravan

I'm fascinated by the key human skills involved in creativity and design thinking. What's even more interesting is that these skills are well taught through observing how bees work with their group intelligence. Bees and their hive mindset offer profound insights into collaborative problem solving, adaptability, simplicity and efficiency, all of which are critical to both creativity and design thinking. By observing how bees work collectively, communicate, iterate and manage resources, we can foster more innovative and sustainable approaches to the challenges we face in human-centred design processes.

Another takeaway for me from this is that the conversation with Toni came about because I'd stopped for long enough to listen to her story of shopping and buying flowers that helped the bees. In those few moments of empathy, I was led to explore more about bees and later to read a book that helped greatly in understanding that the key competencies of creativity and design thinking are human skills, even if they're demonstrated through the example of bees! Thank you, Toni, Siobhán and the bees.

As the anonymous quote goes, 'Anyone who has thought they were too small to make a difference has never met the honeybee.'

Chapter 18

Cross-cultural understanding

My Irish forefathers were not always welcomed into countries to which they emigrated. They were treated suspiciously and largely misunderstood. In time, their contribution and integration enriched many of the same countries that initially offered a cold welcome at best. When people engage in cross-cultural understanding, they're less likely to view their own culture as superior.

The Troubles in Northern Ireland, which escalated in the late 1960s and into the 1970s, were primarily driven by deep-rooted cultural, religious, political and nationalistic differences between two main communities: Unionists/Protestants and Nationalists/Catholics. These differences shaped the conflict, contributing to decades of violence, political instability and social unrest. The Protestant community, which was generally loyal to the British Crown and wanted Northern Ireland to remain part of the United Kingdom, identified primarily as British. They viewed themselves as defenders of a Protestant British identity and were often deeply suspicious of Catholicism and Irish nationalism. The Catholic community, which identified as Irish, largely favoured the unification of Northern Ireland with the Republic of Ireland. Many Catholics felt politically, socially and economically marginalised in Northern Ireland, and they were discriminated against by the Protestant majority and under British governance.

In the decades leading up to the Troubles, Catholics in Northern Ireland faced widespread discrimination in areas such as housing, employment and voting rights. Many public services and government institutions were controlled by the Protestant majority, which favoured Protestant citizens. This marginalisation created a sense of injustice among the Catholic community and contributed to rising tensions. Although both sides of the community were working class, there were wide cultural differences related to British or Irish identities. The 1970s, 1980s and 1990s saw these cultural issues escalate into violence and killings of many in what were dark days for Ireland. Irish people living in the UK were often under suspicion from many British citizens.

The island of Ireland, both in the Republic of Ireland and Northern Ireland, has demonstrated significant leadership in cultural and conflict resolution, particularly in the context of the Good Friday Agreement signed in 1998. As outlined in Chapter 10, the process that led to this peace agreement and its subsequent implementation has been globally regarded as a model for conflict resolution and reconciliation. At the core of the process was building structures that promote cross-cultural understanding, creating opportunities for people from different cultures to work together in ways that avoid miscommunication and misinterpretation. This was central to forging relationships beyond cultural barriers, the benefits of which can be seen today through integrated education. This work is still ongoing but its possibilities should motivate us to ensure that we have proactive and impactful programmes in place at a time when we're globally obliged to play our part in the responsible welcoming of other cultures to our developed countries. As Ireland continues to navigate through demographic changes, weaving different cultures into its own, it has an opportunity to build structures in which cross-cultural understanding is critical.

Closer to home

While we're thankful that the era referred to as the Troubles is behind us, in recent years Ireland has seen the growth of another cultural issue. The country has seen increasing divisions regarding the housing of immigrants, particularly as the country has faced a growing housing crisis. The debate around this issue involves a complex mix of concerns over immigration, social services and housing shortages. While Ireland has traditionally been seen as a welcoming nation for immigrants and asylum seekers, rising pressures on housing and public services have led to increased tensions in some parts of the country.

In my own area of Donegal, some express concerns about the integration of immigrants, particularly in rural communities that have traditionally been predominantly native Irish. The rapid influx of immigrants and refugees, especially from conflict zones such as Syria, Afghanistan and more recently Ukraine, has led to fears that local services, particularly housing, healthcare and education, will be overwhelmed. There's also anxiety about the cultural changes that new populations may bring to small, tightly knit communities – and although they're uncommon, incidents of physical attacks on immigrants have taken place. While Ireland has historically been a more pro-immigrant society than many other European countries, recent years have seen the emergence of a vocal anti-immigrant sentiment, often driven by populist political movements and online misinformation. These groups argue that Ireland should focus on solving its internal housing problems before accommodating more immigrants or refugees. Some fringe groups have attempted to use the housing crisis as a rallying point to push anti-immigrant and other agendas. This is a worrying trend but, and without making light of our national housing problem, I believe the Ireland we wish to build is one in which those fleeing wars and displacements are treated with nothing but respect and dignity as we work on the longer-term solutions of integration for our immigrants.

Musings from Madonna's Caravan

As part of the well-run Donegal Enterprise week, I was recently asked to chair a discussion on engineering. We have a vibrant and growing engineering sector and one that employs more than 2,000 people, and a strong export market tapping into the products being manufactured as well as the services being provided out of Donegal. In the run-up to the conference, I spoke to many owners and managers in the sector to find out more about engineering in Donegal and the challenges they faced. One issue that kept coming up was the recruitment of qualified staff and the inability to grow without good recruitment and retention. More than 100 people attended the short conference but there were only six women in the room. After further questioning, we established that only two of them were engineers and four were administrators.

At the time of writing this chapter, almost 8,000 Ukrainian refugees are living in Donegal. The majority, approximately 70 per cent, are female, and 66 per cent of those have university degrees, many in STEM subjects. Our local Atlantic Technological University currently offers a series of engineering-related courses that could accommodate and encourage our Ukrainian population to upskill and fill the many roles available in engineering. This would narrow the gender inequality gap and also help with the cultural integration of the Ukrainian community into meaningful work in a sector that's challenged by the recruitment of qualified staff. There are similar opportunities in retail, tourism and hospitality, which Ireland relies on greatly and are likewise in difficulty when it comes to staff availability.

Initiating cross-cultural understanding for immigrants involves the provision of accommodation as a basic need, fostering an environment of mutual respect, empathy and shared learning so that they feel safe and valued. Providing language classes not only helps immigrants to learn the local language but also encourages communication across cultural barriers. Offering orientation on local customs, social norms and values can help immigrants integrate, feel more comfortable in their new environment and improve their understanding of local culture. Once these basic needs are met, those who are now settled immigrants can be offered additional education, skills development and opportunities to meet their aspirations for a better life at a time when their contribution is needed in many sectors. A sense of belonging is then achieved.

Chapter 19

Resilience

Resilience is widely considered to be an important human skill. It's defined as the ability to adapt and recover from adversity, challenges or significant stress. While resilience is often seen as an inherent trait, it can also be developed and strengthened through practice, making it a valuable skill in both personal and professional contexts.

In the workplace, resilience contributes to:

→ **emotional regulation** – managing stress and maintaining composure under pressure

→ **problem solving** – finding solutions in challenging situations

→ **adaptability** – adjusting to changes such as new technologies or work environments

→ **team dynamics** – supporting others and fostering a positive attitude within teams.

In our personal lives, resilience is required to overcome crises that occur or traumatic events that have the capacity to change lives in seconds. Trauma presents itself in many ways and recovery can be immediate but is more often slow and continues over a long period of time. As part of the broader set of human skills, resilience also complements other skills such as communication, empathy and adaptability.

The idea that younger generations are less resilient than the previous ones is a common topic of debate, but it's not a straightforward one. It depends on how resilience is measured, the context and the challenges faced by different generations. Studies indicate that anxiety, depression and other mental health issues are more prevalent among younger generations. This could be seen as a sign of reduced resilience, but it may also reflect greater awareness and willingness to seek help, whereas previous generations may have ignored the existence of trauma or suffered through the pain of it without intervention. However, critics argue that certain parenting styles have shielded younger generations from failure, making them less prepared to handle adversity.

Generational resilience is influenced by many factors. Rather than labelling one generation as more or less resilient, it may be better to recognise that each faces distinct challenges and develops resilience in different ways. I try to navigate away from creating a picture that the older generations were tougher and more resilient and that recent generations are less able to bounce back. I've encountered older people who constantly complain about the simplest of things and witnessed younger people working through complex situations that I'd find very difficult to handle.

I don't believe resilience is a generational skill but

simply one that has changed along with the world we live in. I've often questioned my own resilience, perhaps based on my measurement of not sticking to tasks I didn't like or couldn't add value to. In later years, I realised I've been resilient during periods of depression or anxiety. During these times, and with the help of others, I've been able to weather or shelter from the storm or darkness and find myself back in a place of peace, with resilience as part of the recovery process. 'This too shall pass' is a well-known 12-step recovery mantra, meaning that, even if it feels as if they won't go away, the darker days will pass. For many, 'It's OK not to be OK' has been a much more acceptable space to occupy in recent years. In essence, there will be times when it all seems impossible or overwhelming and things are far from being OK. Resilience seems to be found in that place where you hang on in there, making small and steady steps that, along with a good family or friends and the necessary support, bring us back to a place where things are OK and hope is restored.

Closer to home

On 10 May 1991, Alana, an innocent six-year-old from West Donegal, had been on a school tour with her classmates. But events at her home later that evening would change things forever and, over time, shape her life and that of others. Alana's story is horrific and one that involves domestic violence, a pervasive issue that tragically claims lives every day. Her mother Gloria was killed in a devastating act of violence and I'm sharing Alana's story, with her permission, as a powerful testament to the value of resilience by focusing on how, despite setbacks, she was able to rise above such devastating loss. As we delve into this story, it's crucial to remember that help is available. If you or someone you know is facing domestic violence, please reach out to a domestic abuse helpline or similar organisation.

As Alana waited to be collected by her estranged stepfather with her little brother Joseph, aged three, her mother Gloria packed them some clothes for the weekend. Alana wasn't looking forward to the time with her stepfather. Neither her mum nor Alana were happy about the arrangements. They'd both cried together over it more than once since the separation.

When Alana's stepfather arrived and the children were secured in the car, they were sternly warned to stay put and not move out of their seats. Even though she was familiar with this form of discipline, this particular warning stood out for Alana, as she'd become sensitive to danger. The man who was about to take them for the weekend walked back towards the house and approached the front door. Alana could see the conversation becoming more like an argument and, reading the body language through facial expressions, she then heard raised voices. Her mother and stepfather moved inside, leaving the front door open. Alana had seen a lot and heard even more in the time since this man had come into their lives. She was able to assess, even at six years of age, that something was far from right at that moment.

Alana now takes up the story: 'I hear screams. Yes, I'd heard these screams before but it's not something that ever becomes normal. It causes an acute alertness on top of an overwhelming sense of fear no child should ever be forced to feel. The screams continue. I'm scared. I look at my little brother and look back at the house. Everything looks the same, but things are very different. The screams get louder and this time I know I've never heard that level of terror, that volume, that type of scream before. I look back at my baby brother and then all I can think of is the warning not to leave the car. It was an order!

'I was so scared of that man, but I feel compelled to pass that fear on this occasion because I had to get to my mammy at any cost. I jump out of the car and run to the house. I go past the front door to the hallway and then see a frame in the doorway to the kitchen. I am behind the big monster. Mammy is screaming in excruciating pain, lying on the kitchen floor, and this beast is stabbing her with a knife. There's blood all around my mammy and I shout for him to stop. Startled briefly, he notices me but continues the most gruesome, cruel, inhuman attack that's murdering my beautiful mammy. The knife breaks in Mammy's torso and he reaches for another from the block on the counter and carries on relentlessly. I jump on his back and beat my wee fists down on him, pleading him to stop, crying and screaming.

'He throws me off with little effort. I get past him to Mammy's side. She says in a very low tone, barely able to speak, "Go, get help, get someone." I run out of the door and along the path leading out to the neighbourhood estate. I freeze... I'm at a loss. I don't know anywhere to go or anyone to get like Mammy had asked for. I run back to Mammy's side and ask her, "Who will I get, where will I go?" She mumbles this time, unable to answer me, unable to tell where help is but wanting me to be safe. No more screams, only moans, those moans that haunted my nightmares worse than the screams. It meant things had changed. It meant that my only mammy had been taken from me.'

Young Alana had just witnessed an unbelievably horrific event. How could any child survive this psychologically? To watch your mother or, as she described her, 'my only mammy', killed violently in front of her as she fought in vain to stop the violence and then seek help while in turmoil and terror.

Alana concludes the story of the worst night of her life: 'The details of the time that followed are blurry. The monster was talking on the phone. An ambulance came and took my mammy away. We were looked after by a kind neighbour until a relative, an auntie, came to collect us. In my nanny's house in Dungloe, I remember a quiet house with cousins of my mammy's there that night. I really didn't want them to wash the blood from my shoes. I wondered if that was the last bit of Mammy that would be close to me, I thought, "Please don't take that away." I slept with my doting Nanny [Mammy's mam] that night as I'd often done before. In the early hours, I heard the phone ring and a relative at the bedroom door whispering to tell my poor Nanny the awfully sad news. I pretended I was asleep, which I'd done often on all those nights when I heard the screaming and banging from the "safety" of my bedroom. Mammy was most definitely gone… my only mammy.'

For Alana, life after losing her mother was tough beyond words. Her auntie, Gloria's sister, and her husband, took Alana and her brother into their home and treated them as their own. While there was a lot of grief for all the family, her auntie and uncle did their best to be the parents she needed and give her the security that was vital. Eleven days after her mother's tragic death, Alana had her first holy communion. A day that should have been happy was extremely sad.

Alana has memories of her new surroundings. Playing in the countryside with her cousins, she found that nature helped. She liked cycling. Movement was important and so was nature. Her new school proved to be extremely daunting. It was another huge change. She was welcomed and made new friends, but she was sad, lonely, fearful and confused. She was still only a little girl, after all. Alana spent a good deal of time in her bedroom crying. She spent time writing letters to her killer stepfather, asking why he did it. These letters, soaked in tears, were often ripped up, while some were posted. Writing was important to Alana. She carried the burden of guilt for not being able to get help on that tragic night. The guilt weighed heavy on her gentle, young and loving mind. Although brought up with a religious God, she blamed him as well.

As Alana struggled into her mid-teenage years, she discovered alcohol and later drugs. As her main drug of choice, alcohol gave her a temporary release from the pain of the past and the loneliness of the present. She fell into antisocial behaviour, which didn't sit well with her but the reliance on alcohol brought her to places she'd rather not have been, increasing her self-loathing and anxiety. Suffering from depression from a young age, she made several suicide attempts. The hopelessness of her life and the wish to be with her mammy combined, bringing her to the edge of that permanent ending that tragically happens for many.

As her drinking worsened, a series of unhealthy relationships followed. Her vulnerability was a magnet for the wrong partners. Alana became a mum at 21. A second child followed and Alana credits them for saving her life. Although the destructive drinking continued, she ditched the choice of suicide and harder drugs as she dedicated herself to her children, albeit with the addiction to alcohol taking its grip. Alana knew she was in trouble but also had a drive and an aspiration to be better, for herself and for her children. Several unfinished college courses and a few steady and well-paid jobs were part of her story, with alcohol and attempts to hide her drinking still centre stage. Struggling and unwell yet unable to stop, Alana stood at the turning point and was ready to come ashore and try to live differently. At 28 years of age and some 22 years after that night of horror, Alana would walk into recovery and into the arms of new friends and a family of others who were returning from hell. Alana quickly found faith and hope again. She surrendered herself to a simple programme of recovery. It may be simple, but it's not easy. Alana found exercise a big help – the gym, the movement, the challenge. She got married in recovery and has gone on to have an additional five children – a total of seven children she loves immensely and who love her in return.

Alana brings the rest of the story home: 'I've had several unsuccessful attempts at opening my own business. I'm ambitious but balancing a business start-up with seven children isn't easy. I am, however, blessed to have children. I always craved a sister, another girl beside me, and now I have six daughters beside me and a great little boy. I turned 40 this year and recently closed my most recent business. I had to be honest. I'm grateful to God for my family. I'm back in therapy and not afraid to face and experience my feelings anymore. I'm happy but happiness isn't the absence of problems. Life is good.'

Musings from Madonna's Caravan

Like many, I knew Alana's mother, Gloria McCole. She was at school with us. A gentle soul, she was friendly and smiling. Her sister Irene was in my class. Irene was cheekier and a bit brash, but I know now it was perhaps a front because today she's also a gentle soul. As many in our area do, I remember where I was the morning I heard that Gloria had been murdered. Murder was not commonplace then in West Donegal and murdering someone in front of a six-year-old child was unheard of. The community was stunned.

Twenty years after that tragic night, I met Alana for the first time – a beautiful young mother in her mid-twenties, full of ambition to create a business around food, one of her passions, and full of love for her children. I also felt she was at peace – or at least relative peace. I acknowledged that I remembered the fatal night, and that I knew her mum, but didn't infringe on the story. However, I was to hear about its impact on her the following year.

Alana has changed my perception of a few things. When I feel that I've been through a testing time, her story kicks into gear in my mind and I realise that, in comparison, I haven't experienced anything close to this level of trauma.

I also realise that when Alana talks about starting and closing 'an unsuccessful business', she had seven lovely children and recovered from a terrible experience as well as the disease of addiction, which is hardly an 'unsuccessful' result. Her next business will come in its own time but for now her success is in being a lovely, caring mother, much like the one she continues to grieve. Alana clearly displays the human skill of resilience. Like success, resilience leaves clues. Rest in peace, Gloria McCole.

Chapter 20

Collaboration

It was once a term that might have had negative connotations, but today collaboration is viewed in a community or business setting as being highly positive and, in many ways, essential. It's important to look at where the absence of collaboration can have negative consequences and some of the key issues that can arise. Without collaboration, the diversity of ideas and perspectives is greatly reduced, leading to less innovation. Teams will fall into groupthink and run on old, outdated methods. Those who offer new ideas are often disregarded and those who have been in place, usually for a long time, can too often slow down progress because of the mindset that believes 'that's the way it's always been done'.

In the absence of collaboration, different team members might unknowingly work on the same tasks, wasting time and resources. Isolated groups (silos) form and knowledge sharing slows greatly. Ineffective problem solving is a common occurrence, leading to reduced efficiencies that have a long-term impact. In the absence of collaboration, opportunities for growth and skill development are diminished and this can result in staff feeling that there's little in terms of a career pathway in place. Morale is often impacted and overall, the absence of collaboration can significantly hinder the success of a project, team or organisation, too often with a considerable price to pay.

It's therefore little wonder that collaboration has become an important human skill. The need for its inclusion in education, training and development as well as its named presence in the workplace is gathering momentum and rightly so. Many organisations and businesses will try to collaborate in a reactive manner, yet few have a proactive process that consistently encourages collaboration. Many of us have worked in businesses or been involved in clubs, community groups or other organisations that had either good, bad or indifferent collaboration at play. The benefits of positive collaboration are increasing as organisations work their way through a more complex set of situations driven by digital and technological changes.

Closer to home

The Gaelic Athletic Association is a major sporting and cultural organisation based in Ireland. The grassroots of the association are its clubs, which are dotted across every part of the country as well as overseas, as immigrants brought the games and activities with them when they left Ireland. My home club is Naomh Muire in West Donegal (see also Chapter 4). Founded in 1980, when I was 16, it's one of the youngest clubs in Donegal, as many other clubs have longer histories. Since its foundation, the club has been a big part of my life, from playing Gaelic football to being involved in committee activity, fundraising for development work, helping to improve facilities, watching my sons play and later witnessing my grandchildren take part.

Like any community group, there were problems in the early years. Seldom was there a collaborative plan and growth usually happened because of the goodwill and care of several dedicated and committed local people. In many ways the club stumbled on, occasionally achieving success due to a wave of talented players coming through, only to see years with little on-field success due to a recession-forced path of emigration that saw the best players go overseas to seek work, robbing the club of its talent. Facilities were scant or non-existent. In the early years, you togged out in the boot of a car in the rain. Eventually and with a more diverse range of people getting involved with the club, facilities were built, quite often with personalities clashing and in spite of any culture of collaboration. Again, what seemed to carry the growth of facilities forward was that just enough people were prepared to see a long-term benefit and get on with the work required. Basic changing rooms and a clubhouse were built and the playing pitch was improved.

In 2010, an ambitious plan to develop these facilities even further was put forward. The vision was to create a training area to take the pressure off the frequently used single football pitch, add female dressing rooms due to the increased popularity of women's football, and to look into the feasibility of floodlights to allow games and training to take place in the darker evenings when there was no light after 4.30 pm. The argument was that due to the increased number of children taking part in games, the floodlights would add to playtime. The resistance or counter-argument would centre around affordability as well as feasibility. Would a second pitch, if developed, create more opportunity? Often in the absence of a plan, everyone becomes an expert and too often meetings develop into tense and often horrible squabbles that are difficult to control. This puts ambition in the back seat and makes it difficult to find enough common ground to proceed. It wasn't that the committee members lacked ambition or interest; it was just that the interest was in different areas of their development of choice and therefore groups would form and break off, planning different strategies but not collaboratively.

I'd often been impressed by the five phases concept of a project that requires collaboration – forming, storming, norming, performing and then adjourning. Many projects fail at the storming stage, which is where personalities can collide in the absence of a clear vision or structure. The project to erect floodlights and additional facilities often looked doomed, as many opinions were put forward but perhaps with not enough critical analysis of what was required.

Tom Marry, who lived locally in the club area with his wife Bridget and his two sons, was an electrical contractor in London employing up to 150 people on contracts that included the Olympic Games and Sky TV. Tom had become involved in the underage coaching at the club as his sons were involved, but he was quickly encouraged to give his thoughts on the development plan, and particularly the floodlights, which were his area of expertise. Tom was commuting to London weekly and was a busy man. However, he'd later explain that his business success happened when he brought in someone who created better structures of collaborative working. Prior to that, he was an effective electrical contractor, making a good standard of living and winning decent jobs, but he saw that planning and processes centring on a collaborative culture took his electrical contracting business to another level of success.

Tom agreed to take on the project management of the floodlights and the rest of us carried out our assigned roles. My task, with others, was fundraising, which included researching and applying for government funding as well as sharing the vision locally and raising funds from our many emigrants in a 'buy a bulb for your club' campaign. In Tom's process, we were held to account as opposed to going to club meetings and simply talking about what should be done. There was a clear vision and that was to erect floodlights so that the young of the area had a place to train and play after dark. Once the vision was agreed, collaboration became easier. The fundraisers found their way through the challenges and those tasked with getting the best value of pillars and lights did likewise. Others were good at looking at the planning issues, especially as the club grounds were located in the middle of a special area of conservation. The early signs of collaboration were inspiring.

On a given night, a group of us would visit three or four GAA clubs in Tyrone so that club members could show us their lights and explain the technical side to Tom and others, while those of us fundraising talked to the club members who'd tell us what they went through to raise funds for their own floodlights. We'd return home with a wealth of information and new-found contacts willing on our project. On one visit in Tyrone, as daylight was fading and we'd been given great information, a senior and influential person in GAA funding asked if we could keep an eye out for any holiday homes for sale in West Donegal. The following day, we called him with a direct contact of a house for sale only 200 metres from our club grounds. The sale of the holiday home was agreed within a week, and let's just say that we now had, at the very least, knowledge about where sports funds were available for this and other projects. Collaboration leads to such slices of luck. I'm glad to say that this person and his family enjoyed their holiday home as well as honorary membership of our club for many years.

The structure brought in by Tom Marry was hugely collaborative. It wasn't without its moments but the provision of facilities for the youth of the area and the lights to train and play on darker nights was too big a prize to allow egos to dominate. The compelling and authentic vision was the guiding light, and the structure and procedure were the engine that drove the project. This also created much more than the erection of quality floodlights and new changing facilities. It created a new culture of collaboration in the club. Further facilities were added and our proud, humble yet great club won the Club of the Year award for Donegal in recognition of the outstanding facilities made available to the young people of our area. From absolutely no facilities to the best facilities of all 40 clubs in the county gave me a ringside seat to see how the absence of collaboration slows down or indeed stops progress and where the introduction of collaboration works in a manner that's successful beyond a vision.

Musings from Madonna's Caravan

The concept of forming, storming, norming and performing, first proposed by psychologist Bruce Tuckman in 1965, is often used to identify and make sense of where a collaborative project stands. A fifth stage – adjourning – was added later. The initial excitement and enthusiasm of the forming stage is quickly followed by the storming of ideas and opinions. Storming can be a messy phase where diverse thinking styles and personalities often clash. I've often tried to figure out who or what the problem was, but I wasn't as good at looking at the possibility that I was the problem! Ouch! Although I was certainly not alone, it's true that hard-held views and rigid opinions are the barriers to collaboration. Conceding your own opinion for the greater good is important. I needed to realise this. If the vision of a project is clear and compelling and there are clear goals towards achieving that vision, infighting and toxic behaviour are largely avoided.

Having got it wrong 100 times, my lesson is to listen actively to all opinions, even if you believe them to be 100 per cent wrong. At the very least, the person sharing their thoughts will be heard and that opinion valued, and the benefits can be that the minority opinion may in time be of great value to the project. How consensus is achieved is vital. There's little benefit and a lot of harm in strong voices dominating a decision when the quieter, less-heard voices are drowned out in the process. Trust and respect are vital and neither will be achieved by raised voices or fixed opinions that allow for little dialogue or discussion on alternative views. I had to learn that and I had to fail there many times.

The biggest problems that emerged in our GAA club feuds came from those of us who'd played on the same teams 30 and 40 years prior. We were guilty of wanting too much sameness and familiarity. Too many of us felt that, as long-serving club members, we had a monopoly on what was right and wrong for the club. Often it was neighbours and cousins who clashed most; at least that was my experience. We were wary of diversity or people 'coming in'. However, it was within this diversity that the advantage lived. In the case of our club, it was new voices, new styles, different backgrounds that added value. Yes, we could have former players involved in decisions but not a full room of them dominating decisions at the exclusion of others. Along came women's football and that added diversity to the way in which decisions were made. Again, it wasn't plain sailing, but it seldom is, and being comfortable with being uncomfortable is part of the process of accepting change and embedding collaboration. It was and can be a painful process. Change is difficult in the beginning, messy in the middle, yet worth it in the end.

During this transformation of my behaviour within the confines of the GAA club, two life-changing events occurred. The first was studying for a master's degree in leadership and innovation and the other was a serious heart attack. It was a most fascinating time of learning and development, and I mean that seriously. While all of

Collaboration

this was happening and I was recovering from a quadruple bypass, I was also running a business in which I was self-employed, which is a blood sport at times. On reflection, a lot of learning happened in a short space of time. I realised that on my own I'm nothing and that when I needed a serious intervention to keep myself alive, I'd have to trust in a process I knew nothing about, that of open-heart surgery. The process would be in the hands of people I didn't know and had never met before, from Mr Verasingham the surgeon to ambulance drivers, the anaesthetist, doctors, nurses, physiotherapists and hospital porters, all combining through this highly collaborative process to give me a chance to live on, something denied to many.

The primary goal of the clinical team was the successful completion of the surgery and the patient's wellbeing. The vision was clear and every team member was aligned with this purpose. It was a highly diverse team of different nationalities with different skills who relied on each other. The surgical skills of Mr Verasingham and his team were only useful if the nurses and physiotherapist could get my lungs and other organs working again in the critical days after the surgery. Family and friends played a huge role in this recovery. Acts of simple kindness were like medicine. Recovery was not mine; it was a team collaborating without ego or selfishness to restore me to health. Collaboration saved my life.

As I write this chapter overlooking the Boat Strand in Carrickfinn, Donegal, I do so in the hope that the practice of collaboration is something that can be advanced in the workplace, community and indeed at home. I'm quite limited in what I can do alone, but with a collaborative team working towards a compelling vision, much can be achieved. I get to write down my thoughts but also to help companies consider collaboration in their learning and development programmes. As a benefactor of collaboration, gratitude inspires me to share its importance.

Summary

The Irish wake, the greatest show on Earth

My 94-year-old mother died during the writing of this book. The tradition in Donegal is to have a wake for two nights and the burial or funeral on the third day. My father died two years ago, aged 93. Both were from West Donegal. They left at 14 to work in Scotland, married in their twenties, went to the US and returned to Donegal many years ago. Both lived at home until the final months of their long and contented lives. It was also during the writing of this book that my 17-year-old cousin, Chloe Boyle, died suddenly and unexpectedly in New York, and I had the honour of travelling to and being at the wake and funeral, a tradition that carried from Ireland across the Atlantic. For the summary of this book, it's therefore easy for me to highlight the importance of human skills as seen through the lens of a family wake and funeral. An Irish wake is a gathering at which friends, family and neighbours come together to honour the deceased and provide solace to the bereaved. Deeply rooted in tradition, it offers profound lessons in human skills, the power of community and group intelligence.

Shared humanity

At its core, an Irish wake is a recognition of our shared humanity. It acknowledges that loss is a universal experience, and by coming together, we remind each other that no one has to face grief alone.

The power of storytelling

Stories about my mother and young Chloe were shared at their wakes, often blending laughter and tears. This communal storytelling not only celebrates a life but also creates a bridge between sorrow and joy, helping to ease the burden of grief. Eulogies, stories and memories shared during the wake celebrate the person's life and impact.

Celebration amid sadness

While wakes acknowledge sorrow, they also celebrate life through music, food, a drop or two of drink, and laughter. This balance of mourning and joy shows how life's complexities can coexist and how we can find moments of light even in the darkest times.

Diversity, equality and inclusion

Everyone is welcome at an Irish wake, regardless of how close they were to the deceased. Their religious or cultural background is never an issue. While people from several different nationalities and cultural backgrounds were present at my mother's wake in West Donegal, Chloe's was a multicultural and diverse gathering, such is the nature of the Long Island community in which she lived. This type of wake demonstrates unconditional support and teaches that compassion extends beyond the immediate confines of a particular tradition. It's an inclusive act of humanity.

A sense of continuity

By gathering together, the community reinforces the idea that life goes on and the legacy of the departed continues through the connections they fostered. It sends a powerful message that the community will be here for others when they are bereaved. It also reminds us that death isn't the end and if we bring closure, we can find the strength to carry on.

Teamwork and collaboration

People who are brilliant at certain things seem to turn up at wakes and exhibit amazing strengths, from making tea and sandwiches or setting up temporary lights for the night-time rosary crowd at my mother's wake, to the colour and discipline of the New York Police Department's guard of honour and traffic management at Chloe's funeral, showing respect to Chloe's dad, Tommy, a member of the force. People who might not have met before come together to make the tradition of the wake a poetry-in-motion of teamwork.

Empathy

Irish wakes create an environment where grief is shared, reducing the burden on individuals. Empathy and shared vulnerability strengthen bonds and help individuals through tough times. This fosters an emotionally and psychologically safe place where everyone can express themselves while giving and receiving support.

Shared responsibility and collective ownership

Community members shoulder tasks such as cooking, hosting or providing transport, highlighting the value of collective effort. Local shops provide complimentary boxes of wake house essentials, while neighbours offer to collect family members from airports and buses. For weeks after my mother's funeral, cards arrived from many who were unable to attend and indeed those who'd attended but felt the need to further express their support. The wake allows for people to express themselves and show their strengths.

Passing it on

My mother had 12 grandchildren and many great-grandchildren. They watched the rituals and activities and were included in readings and carrying the gifts so that they too can continue the tradition. As young teenagers, hopefully Chloe's friends will have taken some lessons from the experience of her wake and funeral. These lessons demonstrate how the Irish custom reflects deep human connections, highlighting the importance of shared experiences, emotional intelligence and the strength of

Summary

community bonds. They offer a blueprint for fostering strong, empathetic and inclusive environments in any group setting. Rest in peace, Chloe, Sean and Bríd.

Left: Chloe Boyle (RIP) in Ireland in the summer of 2024, only weeks before her tragic death. Right: my father and mother, Sean and Bríd Boyle, on their wedding day in Glasgow. My father passed away in 2022 and my mother died in 2024.

It's not lost on me that these examples of death bring to life the true value of human skills and their impact. While product knowledge, business acumen and digital competency are important skills of the future, it's still the key human skills that remain the spine of humanity and hence *the* skills of the future. As an example, digital design involves both technical and human skills, but the emphasis on human skills is substantial because the methodology centres around understanding and solving human-centric problems. While there isn't a universally agreed percentage, experts generally estimate that 60–80 per cent of digital design thinking relies on human skills. This means that the human skills experienced at Irish wakes are the same as those required at the forefront of digital disruption and growth.

Let's all take these human skills seriously – *viva la revolución*. Please support the work of the Human Skills Institute in bringing the skills that matter to the people that matter – because everyone matters.

Acknowledgements

I never told my mother that I was writing a book. Having known her for my 60-plus years, I was probably afraid that she'd respond with 'You'll shame us'. The fear of shame was a big thing for that generation, and for many reasons. My father was deep in dementia towards the end of his life but could still recollect stories from his younger years. Because of dementia, my mother and father's final days existed in the past and not the present. With the tools they were given, they were good parents. They left home at 14 to create a better life in Scotland and then America, only returning home to Ireland when they felt confident that their children would find a better life. I acknowledge that, without them, this humble effort of writing a book would never have been possible.

    My thanks go to the many who inspired and encouraged the idea of putting my experience and thoughts down on paper. 'You should write a book' was spoken many times by friends and neighbours as I scribbled a blog on Facebook or LinkedIn. Maybe I was taking a subconscious count of these suggestions in the decision process. I knew that the subject of the book was going to be human skills, and investigated doing a PhD over four years. Thankfully, good and honest university academics whom I approached listened with great patience before suggesting that writing a book may be a better fit. I thank them for that guidance because it was correct. Writing the book has given me, on a personal level, more than a PhD qualification would've done and it also involved other people in the process. I acknowledge all who were cheerleaders during the earlier days of 'Will I or won't I?'

Once I decided on that route, finding a publisher wasn't easy. Finding the right one involves many factors but, as always, intuition is vital. I found Sue Richardson and The Right Book Company through an online search. That led to a Zoom call during the pandemic. I'd made up my mind within the first few minutes of our call and was convinced by the end of it. Why? Because my idea of what the book was going to be and Sue's were a world apart. She asked me to consider a few suggestions, and I knew I could trust her and the process she suggested. My thanks go to Sue and her team, developmental editor Bev Glick and client services director Paul East. God love them for their patience and encouragement. Bev didn't allow me to 'hide in my own story' but was also a constant encouragement, and I thank her for that important balance. She also made sure I didn't get us all arrested or sued, and I learned much from her guidance. Bev was a UK pop journalist in the 1980s who coined the phrase 'the New Romantics'. I'm sure she often felt I was far from being a new romantic as she stumbled across some of the original drafts. *Go raibh maith agat,* Bev (thank you, Bev).

The biggest lesson of writing a book is that it's not one person who writes a book; it's a team sport. I wanted to get help locally with editing and research. Sabrina Sweeney

Acknowledgements

had been a BBC journalist and presenter. I was aware of her as she's the daughter of a distant relative and I approached her after watching clips of her work with the BBC. She was living locally with her two daughters, having moved back from England. With her vast experience in writing, producing and editing, I knew she was the right fit and she was happy to be involved. I needed another type of person alongside Sabrina. I'm not a man of detail – it's an 'allowable weakness'. I needed someone who loved reading with a matching curiosity, who could help to research, read and present back interesting elements of a book or article. There were many suggestions of suitable characters and I spoke to several people, mainly in the UK and Dublin, but didn't find the required personal connection until, one day, I sat down with Sheila Greene, who was working with us in the business. I can't recall the exact conversation, but I knew I'd found the person I required, such was her level of general knowledge and love of reading. She also got the concept of the book. Sheila had the passion and curiosity and her level of interest was sustained throughout the writing process. I'd been at school with Sheila back in the day and lost her on the radar of life until she reappeared as the person alongside Sabrina who has guided me, drunk tea, cracked jokes, scolded me for being late, yet would put on a serious face when required. Sabrina and Sheila have been fun and so helpful, and I wouldn't have got past the halfway line without them. They know what the halfway line is! *Go raibh maith agaibh.*

The good people I've mentioned in each chapter are also to be thanked. There were many who contributed by simply being who they are. Some I've never met, such as the crew of the Arranmore lifeboat who rescued the crew of the stricken Dutch ship in Chapter 15. Others, like Chloe, have passed on, but her parents Tommy and Erina allowed me to include her story. Among the many whom I've included in a chapter is one of my heroes, Alana Conaghan, who watched her beloved mammy, Gloria, murdered in front of her. Alana gave me her permission and trust to tell her story, or a small part of it, in the chapter on resilience. In thanking her, I'll continue to encourage her to write the story of her life soon. She's an exceptional person, and I continue to learn much from her and her story.

Family and friends have been an immense support, some by asking 'How's this bloody book coming on?', some looking to the heavens when it's mentioned and others who were more excited at times than I was. One group of friends, who are more like a tribe, consists of a regular collection of sea swimmers. We meet in cold, wet and warm weather at the Boat Strand in Carrickfinn, West Donegal. They gave me encouragement on mornings when I needed to clear my head or indeed get a lift from somewhere. The power of the collective was in the group. There was no talk of the book and that was what I needed – to leave the book and my other concerns on the shore and get out into the sea regardless of its temperature.

Finally, Toni, my editor-in-chief. Once upon a time, in London, I was thinking of buying a new car but was plagued with guilt about not being worthy. I'd just started 'seeing' Toni Sidonio. She said, 'Buy the car. You deserve it as you work hard.' In many ways it was a life-changing comment, although she wasn't aware of it at the time. Two

Acknowledgements

years ago, when I sat down to discuss the writing of a book and all that was involved, Toni (24 years after that first comment) said, 'Go for it… it will be good for you.' In between those two occasions, we had a son, got married and now live in Mullaghduff. Toni was the first to read every chapter and I learned to read her reaction by what she didn't say as opposed to what she did. It's an Italian trait, I believe. She knows how much she has helped not only here in this book but in my life in general. Her love and care when things were dark mean that my love and thanks are returned in brighter mornings of light. *Grazie mille* (thanks a million).

As it would be impossible to mention everyone individually, I'd like to take this opportunity to thank everyone who contributed in any way. Never underestimate the simple gesture of support and its power to keep someone going. I benefited from that through the writing of this book and for that I'm grateful.

Bibliography

Introduction

Skillnet Ireland (2020) 'Retail Ireland Technologies and Future Skills report' URL: skillnetireland.ie/insights/retail-technologies-and-future-skills-report-retail-ireland-skillnet

Massachusetts Institute of Technology, 'Jameel World Education Lab Human Skills Matrix'. URL: jwel.mit.edu/work/posts/human-skills-matrix

Chapter 1

Heaney, S (1991) 'Markings'. URL: resources.teachnet.ie/ckelly/heaney/Markings.htm

Muireann Bradley's YouTube channel: youtube.com/channel/UCwByJBtJn-lZGuNNm_6CnQQ

Chapter 5

Finders, K (2024) 'Post Office Horizon scandal explained: Everything you need to know'. *Computer Weekly*, 8 December. URL: computerweekly.com/feature/Post-Office-Horizon-scandal-explained-everything-you-need-to-know

The Cloyne Report (2011) RTE News, 13 July. URL: rte.ie/news/2011/0713/303635-cloynetracker

McDonald, H H (2011) 'Catholic clergy "abused children for decades in County Donegal"'. *The Guardian*, 29 August. URL: theguardian.com/world/2011/aug/29/catholic-clergy-children-donegal-report

Murphy, Y (2009) 'Commission of Investigation Report into the Catholic Archdiocese of Dublin'. URL: bishop-accountability.org/reports/2009_11_26_Murphy_Report

Chapter 6

Hume, J (1998) 'Nobel lecture'. The Nobel Prize, 10 December. URL: nobelprize.org/prizes/peace/1998/hume/lecture

Chapter 7

Goleman, D (1995) *Emotional Intelligence: Why it can matter more than IQ*. Bloomsbury Publishing.

Channell, M (2021) 'Daniel Goleman's emotional intelligence in leadership: How to improve motivation in your team'. TSW Training. URL: tsw.co.uk/blog/leadership-and-management/daniel-goleman-emotional-intelligence

Chapter 8

Lencioni, P A (2002) *The Five Dysfunctions of a Team: A leadership fable*. Jossey-Bass Inc.

Cullen, P (2024) 'One-quarter of over-18s say they are neurodivergent or have a family member who is, survey finds'. *The Irish Times*, 22 March. URL: irishtimes.com/health/2024/03/22/one-in-10-adults-describe-themselves-as-neurodivergent-survey-finds

Healy, B (2024) 'Neurodiversity in the US: 19% of Americans identify as neurodivergent'. YouGov US, 14 November. URL: today.yougov.com/health/articles/50950-neurodiversity-neurodivergence-in-united-states-19-percent-americans-identify-neurodivergent-poll

Arranmore Blueway: discoverireland.ie/donegal/arranmore-blueway

Chapter 9

Thomas, K W & Kilmann, R H (1974) 'Thomas–Kilmann Conflict Mode Instrument'. URL: kilmanndiagnostics.com/overview-thomas-kilmann-conflict-mode-instrument-tki

Chapter 10

Belbin, R M (1996) 'Team roles and a self-perception inventory'. URL: psycnet.apa.org/record/1997-97002-023

Hughes, D (2018, withdrawn in 2020) *The Barcelona Way: Unlocking the DNA of a winning culture.* Macmillan.

Chapter 11

Dweck, C S (2012) *Mindset: How you can fulfil your potential.* Robinson.

Chapter 12

Mehrabian, A (1971) *Silent Messages: Implicit communication of emotions and attitudes.* Wadsworth Publishing Company.

Morgan, N (2016) 'Mehrabian's myth – speakers,

misinformation, untruths'. Presentation Guru, 20 May. URL: presentation-guru.com/mehrabians-myth

Chapter 13
Robinson, K (2006) 'Do schools kill creativity?' URL: ted.com/talks/sir_ken_robinson_do_schools_kill_creativity

Sinek, S (2009) 'How great leaders inspire action'. URL: ted.com/talks/simon_sinek_how_great_leaders_inspire_action

Chapter 14
WHO (2024) 'Global status report on alcohol and health and treatment of substance use disorders'. URL: who.int/publications/i/item/9789240096745

Chapter 15
Konrath, S H, O'Brien, E H & Hsing, C (2011) 'Changes in dispositional empathy in American college students over time: A meta-analysis'. URL: doi.org/10.1177/1088868310377395

Haidt, J (2024) *The Anxious Generation: How the great rewiring of childhood is causing an epidemic of mental illness.* Allen Lane.

Chapter 16
World Health Organization (2022) 'World mental health report: Transforming mental health for all'. URL: who.int/publications/i/item/9789240049338

Karpman, S (1968) 'Fairy tales and script drama analysis'. *Transactional Analysis Bulletin* 7(26).

Chapter 17

QS World University Rankings 2025: Top global universities. URL: topuniversities.com/world-university-rankings

CREW innovation and enterprise hub: crewdigital.ie

McHale, S (2024) *The Hive Mind at Work: Harnessing the power of group intelligence to create meaningful and lasting change*. HarperCollins Leadership.

Chapter 18

Glenn, L (2024) 'Almost 8,000 people arriving from Ukraine are living in Donegal'. URL: derryjournal.com/news/people/almost-8000-people-arriving-from-ukraine-are-living-in-donegal-4838219

Chapter 19

WHO (2024) 'Mental health of adolescents'. URL: who.int/news-room/fact-sheets/detail/adolescent-mental-health

Domestic abuse support organisations: womensaid.org.uk, mensaid.co.uk

Chapter 20

Stein, J (n.d.) 'Using the stages of team development'. MIT Human Resources. URL: hr.mit.edu/learning-topics/teams/articles/stages-development

Tuckman, B & Jensen, M A (1977) 'Stages of small-group development revisited'. URL: journals.sagepub.com/doi/10.1177/105960117700200404

EU Safety Representative: euComply OÜ Pärnu mnt 139b-14 11317 Tallinn
Estonia hello@eucompliancepartner.com +33 756 90241

www.ingramcontent.com/pod-product-compliance
Lightning Source LLC
Chambersburg PA
CBHW042142160426
43201CB00022B/2370